How Far Does Christian Freedom Go?

How Far Does Christian Freedom Go?

An Exegetical Commentary on First Corinthians Six

By

Spiros Zodhiates, Th.D.

AMG Publishers
Chattanooga, TN 37422

How Far Does Christian Freedom Go?
An Exegetical Commentary on First Corinthians Six

ISBN 0-89957-465-3

Printed in the United States of America
03 02 01 00 99 98 –A– 7 6 5 4 3 2

To Charles T. "Chuck" Weaver whose diligence in reading and checking the manuscript is deeply appreciated and acknowledged.

Contents

Preface

A born-again believer in Jesus Christ is the freest man or woman one could imagine.

But he voluntarily limits his freedom by becoming a slave of Jesus Christ (Rom. 6:6). His freedom, therefore, is circumscribed by what will please his Master, the Lord Jesus Christ.

In the utilization of his freedom, the Christian says, I will not do whatever I have the right to do, but only what will please my Lord.

This is the apostle Paul's concern in 1 Corinthians 6. It is difficult to understand what Paul describes as the freedom of the Christian if one does not fully understand the words that he uses in the Greek in which he wrote this chapter and the rest of 1 Corinthians.

There is only one thing a person can do in order to become a new creature in Christ Jesus. He must believe on Christ and then he will receive eternal life. But when there are choices to make between that which is permissible but not excellent for his personal growth and for an exemplary behavior before others, then his choice becomes a difficult problem. This is why Paul wrote 1 Corinthians 6. He wants to guide us in the choices that we make in our life of belief. These choices will have consequences over which we have no control. I hope that from this book we shall learn to consider the consequences before we make the choices. This is the challenge of 1 Corinthians. Paul's message is that the Christian has duties rather than rights and the performance of these duties brings joy. Diligence in doing one's duties affects not only his own life, but the lives of others.

As you study 1 Corinthians 6 and come to the end of it, you will cry out, "Not what is my right to do, but what is my duty to do as a child of God."

It is with this prayer that I send forth these studies on 1 Corinthians 6. You will be spiritually richer for studying them carefully.

SPIROS ZODHIATES

"Man makes the choices, but God sets the consequences."

An Overview of First Corinthians

Author:	Paul the apostle, author of thirteen other Epistles to various individuals and congregations.
Date:	About A.D. 55.
Recipients:	The congregation Paul had established in Corinth.
Place:	From Ephesus.
Theme:	Paul had received news about the Corinthian brethren from several sources (1 Cor. 1:11; 7:1; 16:17). The church was afflicted with many of the problems that face young churches and new converts. The apostle, under the inspiration of the Holy Spirit, decided to write this urgent letter to admonish and instruct the church. Among other topics he discussed: the necessity of church discipline (5:1–13); divisions and disputes among Christians (1:10–16; 6:1–11); matters of conscience (8:1–13; 10:19–33); the support of preachers (9:1–27); abuses of the Lord's Supper (10:16–17, 21; 11:17–34); the misuse of spiritual gifts (12:1—14:40); and the importance of the resurrection of Jesus Christ (15:1–58).

An Outline of First Corinthians

In the days of the apostle Paul, Corinth was the capital city of the Roman province of Achaia and the glory of Greece. Though its great ancient splendor had been destroyed by the Romans in 120 B.C., the city was rebuilt under Julius Caesar and restored to wealth and luxury under Augustus. Among all the cities of the world, however, it was most well known for its lewdness. The apostle Paul lived in Corinth for eighteen months (Acts 18:11). After his departure, Paul went to Ephesus. During his three-year stay there, he heard reports of wickedness and division within the Corinthian church. In an effort to correct these evils, Paul wrote several letters to them, including the epistle of First Corinthians.

1:1–9	The introductory remarks of Paul.
1:10–16	Paul condemns the divisions in the church and exhorts its members to unity.
1:17—2:16	Paul defends his ministry. He has preached the wisdom of Christ crucified. This wisdom is foolishness to the world, but is the glory of all those to whom the Spirit of God has revealed the truthfulness of it.
3:1–5	Paul declares that the simplicity of his teaching was due to the carnal state of the Corinthians, which state is clearly evidenced by their divisions.
3:6–23	Jesus Christ is the only foundation. Ministers are mere servants; the work is God's.
4:1–6	The duty of ministers is faithfulness.
4:6–21	Paul contrasts the arrogance and conceit of the false teachers to the humility and sacrifice of the apostles. Using his unique position as their spiritual father, Paul calls on the Corinthian believers to be discerning.
5:1–13	Flagrant, sexual immorality was being practiced by one of the members of the congregation. Paul reproves

	their lack of discipline and calls for expulsion of the guilty party.
6:1–11	Christians should not bring their legal disputes before heathen judges.
6:12–20	Paul reprimands the perversion of the principle of Christian liberty to excuse fornication. Our bodies belong to the Lord and should be devoted to His glory.
7:1–17	Paul answers their questions about marriage.
7:18–24	Paul advises that, provided they are not immoral or unlawful, our social positions should remain intact after coming to Christ.
7:25–40	Paul answers their questions about virgins and widows.
8:1–13	Christian liberty and conscience: was it lawful to eat meat that had been sacrificed to false gods?
9:1–23	Paul declares the right of ministers to be faithfully supported by their congregation.
9:24—10:13	Exhortations to self-denial.
10:14—11:1	While the purchase of meat offered to idols is a matter of conscience, attendance at the heathen feasts of sacrifice is idolatry, even if such was not their intention.
11:2–16	Men and women should take care to conform to the customs of dress in their community that assure modesty and properly reflect the man to be "the glory of God" and the woman to be "the glory of the man."
11:17–34	Paul exhorts the Corinthians to properly partake of the Lord's Supper.
12:1–31	Paul answers their questions about spiritual gifts. He reminds them that they are all members of one body. God has distributed these gifts so that each member may perform the function it is designed for.

13:1–13	Love [*agápe* {26}] is superior to all other gifts.
14:1–25	The gift of prophecy is more valuable than the gift of tongues.
14:26–40	Principles for orderly public worship.
15:1–34	Paul proves the fact of the resurrection of Christ. It is the foundation of our faith and the surety of our own resurrection.
15:35–58	Paul explains the nature of our resurrection.
16:1–9	Paul's specific instructions for the collection of monies from several Greek congregations for the poverty-stricken saints in Palestine.
16:10–12	Recommendations for Timothy and Apollos to be accepted by the Corinthians.
16:13–24	Paul's final admonition to them to stand firm in the faith. Salutation.

1 Cor. 6:1 | Solving Personal Disagreements with Fellow Believers

Dares one of you, having a matter against another who differs with him, go to law before the unjust and not before the saints?

As a believer, it is a fallacy to think that just because we belong to the family of God, every other believer will agree with us. We must be realistic. Belonging to the body of Christ does not mean that all the other members of the body have the same mindset or the same function. On reading 1 Corinthians 12:12–27, it becomes evident that not all the members of the body of Christ are the same; however, they do complement each other. As in the physical body, its members are different and have different functions, so in the spiritual. Imagine if the body were one big nose!

Christian Unity in Diversity

There is a certain unity in diversity. Paul summarizes his thesis on the body of Christ in verse 27 by saying, "Now you are the body of Christ, and members in particular." Without each individual, the body would be incomplete. But as in the physical world, each person is a discernible and identifiable individual, and yet each one belongs to the same human race. And it is God who made the members of His family all different. It is not **what** makes each person different, but **who** makes them different. This is stressed in 1 Corinthians 4:7, "For who makes you to differ from another?"

Is it not interesting that God made all humans with two ears, two eyes, and one mouth and nose and yet they are so different? It is a good thing they are different, for how else could we identify one another! The Lord made us all of one blood (Acts 17:26), and yet so diverse. No one other than God could create diversity within uniformity in such a consistent manner.

A Physical and Spiritual Phenomenon

This same thing which is true in the physical world is also true in the spiritual world. When we were born again, we became different than we were before. We acquired the characteristics of the new birth, which are easily discernible. "Whoever is born of God does not commit sin; for his seed remains in him: and he cannot sin, because he is born of God. In this the children of God are manifest, and the children of the devil: whoever does not do righteousness is not of God, neither he that does not love his brother" (1 John 3:9, 10). God indwells us and His life is evident in us. A fellow believer recognizes Christ in us; nonbelievers do not, because they have not experientially known Him.

We find in our Christian life that, while believers belong to the same body of Christ, they each maintain their individuality with its own idiosyncrasies. They have the mind of Christ in general, but in each it may be different in its details from other Christians.

There was a Christian who worked in a factory. The other men were unbelievers. They noticed, however, certain differences in his life. He did not curse as the majority did, and whenever the opportunity arose, he would speak of Christ. One day as he was eating his lunch, one of the men asked him, "May I sit by you, Bob? There is a question I have wanted to ask you for some time, but I was hesitant to do it. I want to know what makes you different from the rest of us. You never get angry, no matter what we rough fellows do or say to you. What do you have that we don't have?" The believer replied, "I am no better than anyone else, but Christ is in my heart. He enables me to live differently from others. To Him be the glory!"

During the Second World War, a Christian soldier in the Pacific tells of being caught by surprise while unarmed by a Japanese soldier who suddenly emerged from the jungle. Completely at the mercy of his captor, he felt his life was about to be snuffed out when the Japanese suddenly said in broken English, with a smile, "Me Christian. Don't be afraid," and the American was spared. They had something in common.

To Whom Should a Believer Go When He Has a Difference With a Fellow Believer?

"Dares one of you, having a matter against another who differs with him, go to law before the unjust and not before the saints?" The verb "dares" is in the singular (*tolmá*, the third person singular indicative of *tolmáō* [5111], to dare): "Dares any single one [*tis* {5100}, an enclitic indefinite pronoun] of you [*humṓn* {5216}]?" The controversy starts with an individual who differs from another.

When Paul says, "any single one" (*tis*), he does not point a finger at any particular individual. What Paul does say, though, is to allow each one to examine himself.

Is it possible that there is anyone who in all things agrees with everybody in everything? I certainly do not qualify. There are things in which I am different. Paul said in 1 Corinthians 11:1, "Be ye followers of me, even as I also am of Christ."

"Is anyone of you having a matter against another?" That word "another" in Greek is *héteron,* the accusative of *héteros* (2087) which means another but different. This is contrasted to *állos* (243) which means merely another, similar. The definite article is before the word *héteros* to indicate that there is a specific person who is different. You will find someone who is different than you in every Christian church.

What are we to do in such a case? That difference, when concentrated upon, can be magnified so greatly that we are likely to consider it as a threat against our way of living, so much so that we may believe the matter is worth going to court to resolve.

We must remember that secular judges are supposed to render justice, but they themselves are frequently unjust (*ádikoi* [94]), for righteousness is a spiritual quality. We may really be trying to protect not truth as such or a principle of Christian doctrine and practice, but a way of life that we have made a law and expect everyone else to follow. We may consider others to be unspiritual or even dishonest if they do not conform with our idea of model Christian conduct.

Why Unbelieving Judges Are Called Unjust

Scripture concerns itself that a case involving believers be settled by the "saints" of the church. Jesus delineates a settlement in Matthew 18:15–20. We are admonished by Him to keep our differences among believers and resolve them within the church. Let them not spill out, for the world is incapable of judging differences among Christians since they are not spiritually discerning. A secular judge does not understand Christian principles, and the end result will be detrimental to the cause of Christ. It is good for every local church to have an arbitrating group of wise, godly individuals.

LESSONS:

1. Realize that you belong to a Christian brotherhood that possesses a certain group of distinctive principles peculiar to all believers (1 John 2:3, 6, 9–11, 15, 16, 29; 3:6–10, 13–15, 21–24; 4:1, 4–6, 17–21; 5:13, 21).
2. Realize that although you are a Christian, other Christians will not always agree with you in the details of life. Grace is not law. It creates sanctified individuals, but they are still individuals.
3. As individuals, you will be different.
4. Settle differences internally within the Christian church, and do not resort to the secular courts.
5. Judges govern by man-made laws, not Christian standards.
6. The simplest "saint" is better than an intelligent judge who has not experienced Christ's justifying grace.

1 Cor. 6:2 | *The Saints Shall Judge the World*

Do you not perceive that the saints shall judge the world? And if the world is judged by you, are you unworthy to judge the smallest matters?

There may have been some objection on the part of the Christians in Corinth to allow the saints to make decisions as to their differences. Perhaps they claimed they were incompetent.

Who Should Judge Disagreements Among Believers?

Realize that the Christian world is comprised of saints competent to solve differences between believers. Paul meets the possibility of objection head-on. It is true the would-be Christian arbitrators may not have been certified by a law school or by the state to sit in judgment of others. What, therefore, is their qualification for this task?

The Christian lives in two environments simultaneously, the environment of the world, which means the world of unbelievers, and the environment of believers which is the church. The church is autonomous as far as believers are concerned. In our country, generally speaking, nobody from outside of the church will interfere in its differences as long as the matters concerned are strictly interrelationships between believers and do not affect the state or the world outside of the church. Some member of the church must disturb the common good of the community in order for the world to step into the affairs of the church.

However, this was not the case in the Corinthian church with which the apostle Paul is dealing. The case was the difference or complaint that one individual believer had against another believer. It was not a matter of difference in doctrine, but a matter of earthly possessions (*biōtiká* [982], things pertaining to this life [see Luke 21:34]). Simply put, it concerned money differences between believers. Possibly they were engaging in business with one another. Inevitable disagreements arose. Paul was addressing the question as to whether the believers were to have such disputes solved by a judge of the state, who undoubtedly would be an unbeliever, or whether believers within the church should act as the arbitrators of such differences. The objection that naturally arose was whether such believers within the church were competent and whether their decision about the matter should be binding.

The apostle Paul was concerned that the church would be so structured that there would be an acknowledged group within the church with such powers. The most natural group of saints that would function as arbitrators of differences among believers in a church should be the government of that local church, the council of elders. Even the less esteemed believers would qualify for such a duty (v. 4).

The Church Has Its Own Governing Body

In the New Testament we have *tó presbutérion* (4244), the presbytery or the council of elders—*presbúteros* (4245) is an elder. There is always to be a plurality of elders in a local church. Paul in 1 Timothy 4:14 says, "Neglect not the gift that is in you, which was given you by prophecy, with the laying on of the hands of the presbytery." From Acts 20:17–28 it is evident that each local church had a number of elders: "And from Miletus he sent to Ephesus, and called the elders of the church." These elders are also called overseers or bishops (*epískopoi* [1985]). Paul writes, "Take heed therefore unto yourselves, and to all the flock [the local church] over the which the Holy Ghost has made you overseers [*episkópous*], to feed the church of God which He has purchased with His own blood" (v. 28). Along with the elders or bishops were also the deacons (*diákonoi* [1249]) in the local church (Phil. 1:1). However, deacons are never presented as a governing council as are the elders. Their duty is to assist the elders. The word "deacon" is *diákonos* meaning "servant," one who ministers to the needs of others.

It would therefore be logical that any differences among believers be brought before the council of elders, the presbytery. Paul's concern here is not what group in the church acts as the jury, as long as they are not outside the church and unbelievers. They are "the saints" as contrasted to "the unjust" jurors.

Will Believers Judge the World?

Paul then goes on to a general eschatological teaching concerning believers and unbelievers. "Do you not perceive [*ouk* {3756}, the absolute 'not'; *oídate*, the perfect used as a present of *eídō* {1492}, to perceive, to know as a result of your relationship with Christ] that the saints will judge the world?" You know this intuitively, Paul says, because you are believers. Nonbelievers would laugh at such a teaching, since they do not even believe in a world to come. As the world to come is considered by unbelievers to be only a dream of Christians, so is any claim of a future rule over them.

Nevertheless, we know from the Word of God that believers will judge the world. This is first stated in Daniel 7:22 where we read: "Until the Ancient of Days came, and judgment was given to the saints of the Most High; and the time came that the saints possessed the kingdom."

Psalm 49:14 states, "Like sheep they are laid in the grave; death shall feed on them: and the upright [the saints] shall have dominion over them in the morning; and their beauty shall consume in the grave from their dwelling."

In the New Testament we read in Matthew 19:28: "And Jesus said unto them, 'Verily I say unto you, That you who have followed Me, in the regeneration [*paliggenesía* {3824}, restoration] when the Son of man shall sit on the throne of His glory, you also shall sit upon twelve thrones, judging the twelve tribes of Israel.'" The "regeneration" or restoration referred to is the coming state of the whole creation (Rev. 21:1), equivalent to the restoration of all things referred to by Peter in his Pentecostal address (Acts 3:21) which will occur when the Son of Man shall come in His glory (Matt. 25:31).

In Revelation 2:26 John gives the promise of Christ to the overcomers, the saints of the church of Thyatira and by extension to the saints of all the churches (2:23), "And he that overcomes and keeps My words unto the end, to him will I give power over the nations [meaning the heathen, the unbelieving world]."

And to the overcomer of the church of Laodicea and by extension to all the overcomers of all the churches (3:22), the Lord says, "To him that overcomes will I grant to sit with Me in My throne, even as I also overcame, and am set down with My Father in His throne" (Rev. 3:21).

In this present age, the world may imprison and kill the saints. So it will be in the case of the saints who will believe during the tribulation period. But the day is coming in the new world when Revelation 20:4 will be realized and this order will be reversed:

> And I saw thrones, and they sat upon them, and judgment was given unto them. And I saw the souls of them that were beheaded for the witness of Jesus, and for the Word of God, and which had not worshiped the beast [the antichrist], neither his image, neither had received his mark upon their foreheads, or in their hands; and they lived and reigned with Christ a thousand years.

If Believers Will Judge Unbelievers, They Ought to Suffice in Judging Their Fellow Believers Now

Paul maintained that believers within the church should be the judges of other believers who had differences and disputes among themselves. "In what have I to do to judge them also that are without? Do not you judge them that are within?" (1 Cor. 5:12). He implies that it was not his responsibility as an apostle to sit as a judge, but the saints of a local church should solve the inner problems between believers.

Spiritual Yardsticks for Judging Material Matters

Then Paul closes verse 2 with a penetrating question: "And if by you the world is judged [*krínetai,* the present passive indicative of *krínō* {2919}, to judge], are you unworthy of judgments [*kritēríōn,* the genitive of *kritḗrion* {2922}, abilities and standards to make decisions] on matters that are insignificant [*elachístōn* {1646}, the superlative of *mikrós* {3398}, small, the least]?" They are called of least importance because they pertain to material things (*biōtiká,* material things of life). Anything that has to do with earthly things and not with the eternal destiny of the believer is insignificant.

<u>LESSONS</u>:

1. We know that believers will judge the world because Christ assured us that we shall sit with Him on His throne in judgment (Rev. 3:21).

2. We are admonished in this life not to judge our fellow human beings (Matt. 7:1), but in the world to come we shall be the judges.
3. Christians should not consider themselves unworthy and underestimate their ability to solve problems and differences among themselves. Their qualification is divine discernment (1 Cor. 12:10). Their standards are spiritual (2 Cor. 2:14, 15).
4. We must be careful not to allow matters of least importance, material things, to interfere with our spiritual relationships.

1 Cor. 6:3 | Believers Shall Judge Angels

Do you not perceive that we shall judge angels? How much more material things ***that pertain to this life?***

In order to convince the believers in regard to their position of separation from the world and superiority of judgment, Paul gives them a truth such as we find nowhere else in the Word of God: "Do you not perceive [*ouk* {3756}, the absolute 'not'; *oídate,* the perfect used as present indicative of *eídō* {1492}, to perceive, to know intuitively as a result of our relationship with Christ] that we shall judge angels?"

Angels

First we must examine what kind of angels Paul is speaking about. Angels are spiritual beings created by God, without corporeal identity. Although we are not cognizant of them, angels play a significant role in our lives and in the whole course of history. They are ministering spirits sent forth to minister to those who shall be heirs of salvation (Heb. 1:14).

Angels were created by God and were witnesses to the creation of the material universe. They were created in, through, and unto Christ (Col. 1:16), who is the beginning and the end of all things (1 Cor. 8:6). They are not inferior deities, but fellow servants with man (Rev. 19:10; 22:9); therefore, they may not be worshiped. The worship of angels was one of the grave errors at Colossae (Col. 2:18).

In the New Testament, both good and evil angels are mentioned. The good angels serve both God and believers here on earth, and generally the words "angel" or "angels" refer to the good angels who have not fallen.

Fallen Angels

The fall of some angels is mentioned in Jude 1:6: "And the angels which kept not their first estate, but left their own habitation, He has reserved in everlasting chains under darkness unto the judgment of the great day."

In 2 Peter 2:4 we read, "For if God spared not the angels that sinned, but cast them down to hell, and delivered them into chains of darkness, to be reserved unto judgment. . . ." So these fallen angels are being held for final punishment. It is in this judgment of the fallen angels that believers are going to participate. Isaiah 24:21 states, "And it shall come to pass in that day [the day of final judgment] that the Lord shall punish the host of the high ones that are on high [angels], and the kings of the earth upon the earth."

Thus it is the exalted position of believers to someday judge the world (unbelievers) and fallen angels. How, then can we claim that believers are unworthy to judge earthly matters? To demonstrate the insignificance of earthly matters that divide Christians, Paul uses an expression that is used only here in the entire New Testament: "how much more [*mḗtige* {3386}, from *mḗti* {3385} which in turn is made up of *mḗ* {3361}, the relative 'not,' and *ti* {5101}, anything]." The *ge* (1065) is an intensive which means "yet." Since believers are entrusted by God to judge the world and the fallen angels who are kept unto judgment, how much more can we trust them to make judgments pertaining to material things?

What Occasioned Differences Among Believers

These "material things" in verse 3 are expressed with the adjectival noun *biōtiká* (982), things pertaining to the manner of life (*bíos* [979], possessions or wealth). It seems that material possessions separated otherwise loving Christians. A perfect example is the case of Abram and Lot (Gen. 13:2, 5–13). Such differences among believers ought to be resolved among themselves.

LESSONS:

1. The believers are to be entrusted with the high responsibility of judging fallen angels (Jude 1:6).
2. Material matters which are of smaller importance should not be settled in court, but within the church with saints acting as judges. The judgment ought to be accepted as binding.
3. Only believers have the intuitive knowledge of the worthiness of saints in preference to secular judges.

1 Cor. 6:4 | Christians Should Settle Disputes Among Brethren

If then you have standards for material things ***pertaining to this life****, set them* ***to judge*** *who are least esteemed in the church.*

When there is dispute concerning material things, what are the standards to be used in judging who is right and who is wrong?

Apply Spiritual Principles to Solve Material Differences

The standard which determines what is right or what is wrong in a matter is called *kritḗrion* (2922) in Greek, from which we get our English word "criterion." The word comes from *krínō* (2919), to judge, which literally means to distinguish or determine whether it answers to the standard which is truth. *Kritḗrion* can be the means of judging, the place of judgment, or the judgment itself. Here it refers to the means of judgment. "If, then, you have [*eán* {1437}, 'if' as a suppositional conjunction of reality; *échēte*, the present subjunctive of *échō* {2192}, to have] standards," or means of judging the material things of life (*biōtiká* [982]), then you must also have spiritual principles with which to discern attitudes. Paul is saying that even those in the church, in spite of the fact they are despised by the world, would make good judges as long as they have proper standards whereby to judge.

Beware Lest Material Things Bring Divisions

Material things divide not only members within the same family, but also those belonging to God's family. It behooves us to be realists while we live in a material world. We should not behave as belonging to the world. The believer ought to realize that life does not consist in the abundance of the things which he or she possesses (Luke 12:15). This is the answer Jesus gave to someone who came to Him asking Him to be a judge in the division of the inheritance with his brother (Luke 12:13). The Lord further said, "Man, who made me a judge or a divider over you?" (Luke 12:14). In other words, the Lord did not consider it worthwhile to spend His time solving differences relating to material things. And yet this is the cause of so much division between brethren!

What a shame it is for Christians to resort to courts of law to solve their differences over the least important matters, that is, material things. No wonder the Lord gave the stern warning that we should "Take heed and beware of covetousness [*pleonexía* {4124}, the desire to possess more]" (Luke 12:15). He who does not think he has enough and always wants more is miserable. He who thinks his own brethren deprive him of what should belong to him would not hesitate to take them before unjust judges to satisfy his covetousness.

Despised Believers Are Better Than Secular Judges

To solve differences in the local church, we should call upon people who have spiritual principles. These may be considered by the world as abject and despised. They are Christians, nevertheless, whose philosophy of life is radically different from that of the world. Obviously, Paul considers them more capable than unbelieving secular judges. The word for despised Christians is *exouthenēménous*. It comes from *ek* (1537), an intensive, which becomes *ex* because the next word begins with a vowel, and *outhenéō*, to bring to nought or nothing. They are people who do not count for anything. The verb is *exouthenéō* (1848) and the ones who are the least in the world are called thc "despised." Not that they are despised by God, because God is not a respecter of persons (Acts 10:34). The parable of the Pharisee and the publican was spoken by Jesus because there were some who considered themselves just and consequently despised others (Luke 18:9).

In our verse, Paul claims that the despised of the world are in the church. They may be despised and rejected, but they are people of spiritual principles which are often lacking among the noble and educated of the world. Of the Lord it was said "that He must suffer many things, and be set at nought [*exoudenōthḗ*]" (Mark 9:12). Peter, speaking to the priests and Sadducees in the temple, said of Jesus, "This is the stone which was set at nought [*exouthenētheís*] of you builders, which is become the head of the corner" (Acts 4:11).

There should not be difficulty choosing among the despised in a local church, because it pleased God to choose them to be saved. "And base things of the world, and things which are despised [*exouthenēména*] has God chosen, yes, the things which are nothing to bring to nothing things that are" (1 Cor. 1:28).

Therefore, when Paul speaks of the despised in the local church, he does not speak of approving such social and economic distinctions among Christians. Rather, he refers to any Christian believer as being wiser than those who are affluent and powerful in the world. It is God's children of whom John speaks as knowing all things. In 1 John 2:20 he says, "But you have an unction from the Holy One, and you perceive [*oídate* from *eídō* {1492}, to know intuitively, to perceive as a result of being related to God] all things." The despised in any local church are better qualified than the best trained secular judges to advise on matters of possessions among Christians. Do not look down upon the "despised" of men. They are not necessarily despised of God.

". . . Set them *to judge* who are the least esteemed in the church." The Greek text says *toútous kathízete* (*toútous* [5128], these very ones, referring to the despised; *kathízete*, the present imperative of *kathízō* [2523], to cause to sit down). That is all Paul says. He does not say "to judge" as the translation has it. This is implied.

To whom does Paul give this command? Undoubtedly to the saints and the leadership of the Corinthian church. This church must have been as the church in Philippi which had the saints in Christ Jesus, the bishops, and deacons (Phil. 1:1). The bishops are the elders (Acts 14:23; 20:17; 1 Pet. 5:1, 2).

While the least esteemed would not consider themselves competent, give them the esteem they deserve. As Paul said of young Timothy, "Let no man despise him" (1 Cor. 16:11).

LESSONS:

1. Christians ought to have spiritual standards to judge material things.
2. These standards are the fundamental difference between them and unbelievers.
3. Most despised Christians have spiritual principles which judges may lack, but unbelievers will not allow them to apply them in a world that lives in the wicked one (1 John 5:19).
4. Therefore, the most despised in the church are better qualified to render judgment than the greatest judges who are "unjust" inasfar as spiritual truth is concerned.

1 Cor. 6:5 | *We Must Not Shame the Name of Christ*

I speak to your shame. Is it so, that there is not a wise man among you? No, not one that shall be able to judge between his brethren?

Paul appealed to the Christians of Corinth in an attempt to persuade them that when having differences one with another, not to resort to unbelieving judges. After telling them that it is better to find despised believers and appoint them to act as judges, he said, "I speak to your shame." Paul was attempting to arouse them to shame. The word that he used for "shame" is the word *entropḗ* (1791) from the verb *entrépō* (1788), to withdraw. This comes from the preposition *en* (1722), in or inward, and *trépō*, to turn. The meaning is withdrawal for the purpose of reflection and self-examination. It occurs here in 1 Corinthians 6:5 for the first time.

Don't Hang Out Your Dirty Clothes Before Unbelievers

Paul wanted the believers, as Christians, to think what their actions of airing their covetous ambitions before unbelieving judges would imply. The first conclusion that would be drawn is that Christians are no different than non-Christians. Material possessions would be considered to be first in their lives just like everybody else.

Paul, in writing to the Corinthians, reminded them of his own actions in the 18 months he was among them. In 2 Corinthians 7:2 he wrote: "Receive us; we have wronged no man, we have corrupted no man, we have defrauded [*epleonektḗsamen*, the aorist of the verb *pleonektéō* {4122}, to be greedy, to desire to have more material things] no man." The Corinthians were suing other Christians concerning possessions (*biōtiká* [982], mentioned also in vv. 3, 4). To be covetous was inconsistent with Christian living. In verse 10 Paul warns them that the covetous along with other sinners will not inherit the kingdom of God. What kind of a testimony would they be when, for the sake of mere material possessions, they would resort to secular judges? It would bring shame to the gospel.

Paul's message to the Corinthian Christians purposed to prevent them from doing anything that would disgrace the name of Christ. It seems that they had not yet resorted to secular courts, but that they were in danger of doing it. This is indicated by the preposition *prós* (4314), toward, expressing the aim or purpose. It does not imply something done already, but something to be avoided altogether. Paul's letter was designed to make the believers think. It was preventive advice.

Think Before You Act

The noun *entropḗ*, shame that causes reflection, a turning inward or withdrawal, is one of only three words in Greek which can be translated "shame." Another is *aischúnē* (152), shame from a sense of one's wrong action or motive having been made manifest. The third word is *aidṓs* (127), modesty from a sense of what is right and becoming. It is the shame that comes from a sense of what one's conduct should be. Of the three words, Paul chose *entropḗ* which means reflection lest shame should be brought upon the cause of Christ as represented by the local Christian community.

This is the principle which is enunciated by Paul in verse 12: "All things are permissible for me, but not all things are expedient." While the believer may be free to do certain things, such as going to court over a difference with a brother, this is not for the common good (*sumphérei* [4851], for the common advantage, to bring together). One may gain materially by pursuing his personal rights, but this may be detrimental to the community of believers and to the cause of Christ. Therefore, when taking into account this consideration, the believer may decide that the pursuit of personal rights is not for the common good and the glory of God.

An Ounce of Divine Wisdom Is Better Than a Ton of Worldly Knowledge

"Thus [*hoútōs* {3779}, the result of inner reflection as to the consequences of pursuing one's rights] is there not a wise person among you?" The "not" is expressed by the absolute negative *ouk* (3756) as if to indicate that such an eventuality is impossible. In every assembly there must be at least one wise man who can resolve such differences between believers.

"Is there [*éni* {1762} for *énesti*, from *en*, in, and the *i* in *estí*, 'is,' the third person present indicative of *eimí* {1510}, to be] in your church not a wise man?" Paul implies incredulity here to ask, Do you go outside the church because you cannot find a wise person among you to solve your differences? It is impossible to make that assumption!

Very carefully Paul chose the Greek word "wise" (*sophós* [4680]). The biblical concept of wisdom is God-centered rather than man-centered. It denotes a fear of God and an understanding of His ways which certainly was absent among pagan judges. Wisdom (*sophía* [4678]) signifies the possession of certain adeptness or practical ability, not necessarily brilliance or scholastic training. It indicates adroitness, the ability to apply with skill what one knows, especially spiritual truth. See *The Complete Word Study Dictionary: New Testament*, pp. 1301, 1302. John describes such a wise person in 1 John 2:20 when he says of believers, "But you have an unction from the Holy One, and you perceive [*oídate* {1492}, to perceive as a result of your relationship with Christ] all things." Among the "all things" is the ability to solve differences between brethren.

"Wise man" or person here is the predicate making the sentence read, "Thus is there not at all one single person among you who is a wise person?" that is, one who knows the Word of God and can be made sufficiently acquainted with the case that he would render a correct judgment?

The Majority Text and the Textus Receptus have the word "wise" preceding "not even one" (*oudé* [3761], not even, derived from the absolute "not" [*ou*] and the adversative particle *dé* [1161], but, even). The Nestle's Text has *oudeís* which is the abbreviated form of *oudé*, not even, and *heís* (1520), one. However, it does not provide the same emphasis as the two words *oudé eís*. The whole sentence provides a pitiful conclusion as to why the believers in the Corinthian Church looked for a solution outside of the church for an internal problem: "Thus is there not in your midst a person who is wise, not even one who shall be able to discern between the complainer and his brother?"

"Among you" is *en humín* (*en*, among, in; *humín* [5213], the dative personal pronoun plural of *sú* [4771], you). It refers to those within the church, among the brethren. Paul was anxious that differences in the local church be resolved within the church itself. No appeal was to be made to those without (1 Cor. 5:4, 5).

Discernment Is a Spiritual Gift for Believers Only

What is translated "that shall be able to judge" or "discern" is *dunḗsetai* (the third person singular middle deponent indicative of *dúnamai* [1410], to be able, which implies bringing the matter to a satisfactory conclusion; *diakrínai* [1252], to judge). This shows that this one wise person should be found to resolve the matter at hand, although not to be appointed judge of all such matters. "To judge" translates *diakrínai*, the aorist active infinitive of *diakrínō*, to distinguish, derived from the preposition *diá* (1223), through, and *krínō* (2919), to judge, separate. *Diakrínō* is to see through the matter that separates brother from brother. It is not simply to judge who is right and who is wrong. Rather, it is to discern the situation and avert the matter from being referred to outside determination that may be detrimental to the cause of Christ and the testimony of the local church.

The noun of the verb *diakrínō,* to discern, to judge through, is *diákrisis* (1253), discernment. It is one of the gifts which the triune God distributes to believers as mentioned in 1 Corinthians 12:10: "to another discernings of spirits." These are the spirits of men, the motivators of actions. When a brother is moved to sue a fellow believer, he is motivated by a spirit of selfishness or covetousness. The wise person who is to be sought in the local church should have the ability to discern not only what is right or wrong by the action, but what motivates it. A secular judge will determine whether something is wrong in its execution, whereas a wise Christian has the ability to determine why an action has been taken against another brother. He is to discern if it is selfishness or greed, an attitude which should be corrected, not simply a misunderstanding between spiritual brethren.

The expression translated "between his brethren" in Greek is *aná* (303), on or upon; *méson* (3319), in the midst, between; *toú* (3588), of the; *adelphoú* (80), brother; *autoú* (847), his. The wise man is to determine and arbitrate the problem between one brother and another which is leading them to resort to worldly, secular judges for solution.

LESSONS:

1. Christians are free to choose their actions, but, before they choose, they ought to think of the consequences of their choice.
2. If we seriously consider the consequences, we would not do certain things, although we may have the right to do them.
3. In every congregation there is surely someone who has the wisdom or the mind of God to judge between brethren.
4. It is shameful and harmful to the cause of Christ to bring our problems to worldly people to resolve.

1 Cor. 6:6

We Are to Solve Differences among Ourselves

But brother goes to law with brother, and that before unbelievers.

Paul now deals with such an unlikely supposition of not finding a wise Christian to judge a matter between spiritual brothers: "But brother with brother is judged, and this before unbelievers," meaning unbelieving judges. Although a brother in Christ may have a different view about a certain matter than another brother, that does not make him cease to be a brother. This portion of Scripture does not concern a matter of faith or doctrine, but possessions (*biōtiká* [982], things pertaining to the present existence).

The Difference Between Matthew 18:1–20 and 1 Corinthians 6:1–8

This is an entirely different matter than that discussed in Matthew 18:1–20. Our Lord says in Matthew 18:15 that "If your brother shall trespass against you, go tell him his fault between you and him alone. If he shall hear you, you have gained your brother." We are then admonished to invite two witnesses and ultimately bring the matter before the entire church. Only in the case when he disobeys the entire church is the brother to be treated "as a heathen and a publican." The word "heathen" would categorize the evil as doctrinal, and "publican" would categorize the evil as moral.

In 1 Corinthians 6 it is clear that the difference involved between two brothers is an individual difference pertaining to possessions. For instance, two Christian brothers may have had the relationship of employer and employee, and the difference may be that of wages. That difference should never be brought before the entire church, but should be solved by one or more individual fellow believers.

Recognize Secular Judges as Unbelievers

Such differences may never be brought to secular courts. The reason for this, as verse 1 says, is that such judges are *ádikoi* (94), unrighteous or unjust. They do not possess the righteousness of God. In Romans 3:22 Paul tells us that "the righteousness of God which is by faith of Jesus Christ unto all and upon all them that believe." In 1 Corinthians 6:6 the same judges who in verse 1 are called *ádikoi*, unjust, unrighteous, are also called *ápistoi* (571), without faith, meaning the faith of Jesus Christ. Paul is here affirming that there can be no true righteousness rendered where there is no faith of Jesus Christ. Faith in Jesus Christ gives a different sense of righteousness than the world gives.

Paul is not addressing the subject matter of the dispute or who is right and who is wrong, but he asserts that it is wrong for one brother to take another brother to court. There is enough defamation of Christianity. To show that there is disunity in the body of Christ is an evil that is to be avoided. We are enjoined to solve our differences among ourselves. We are members of the same body, the body of Christ.

LESSONS:

1. The case discussed here does not involve the Christian defending himself against a plaintiff who is an unbeliever.
2. What is to be avoided before secular courts is one believer suing another in regard to material things.

1 Cor. 6:7 | *Do Not Become a Defeated Christian*

Now, therefore, there is utterly a defeat among you, because you go to law ***one believer*** *with another. Why do you not rather have wrong done to yourselves? Why do you not rather suffer yourselves to be defrauded?*

Paul now arrives at certain general conclusions concerning a brother going to court against another brother.

A Believer Who Resorts to Secular Courts Is Already a Defeated Christian

The first thing that must be determined is that these believers were under no compulsion to go to court. It was not a matter of an unbeliever suing a Christian who must defend himself. Nor was it the case of a believer suing an unbeliever. It was strictly the case of a believer suing a fellow believer to demand, by the application of the law of the land, a material right or a debt to be paid. It was, quite possibly, a disagreement as to certain financial dealings or, perhaps, property of some kind.

When you have a lawsuit among yourselves, Paul wrote the Corinthian Christians, that in itself must be considered as a defeat (*hḗttēma* [2275], failure, fault). We have translated the adverb *hólōs* (3654), wholly, as "utterly," because when Christians cannot resolve problems among themselves, it is indeed a total defeat. There should not be any cases of dissension which have to be resolved by state courts. This in itself is a complete defeat, and no one is a winner in such a case.

Personal Suffering Is a Greater Victory Than Winning Against Your Brother

And then comes the challenge of the apostle Paul: "Why do you not rather have wrong [*adikeísthe*, the present passive indicative of *adikéō* {91}, to commit an injustice] done to yourselves?" The verb is the present indicative passive which renders it as a general principle. Thus the code of conduct Paul is endeavoring to establish is that it is better for the Christian to suffer injustice than to go to court or enter into public dispute against his brother.

And the second question Paul asks is, "Why do you not suffer yourselves to be defrauded?" The Greek verb is *apostereísthe*, the present indicative passive of *aposteréō* (650), to deprive, defraud. It means to allow yourself to be deprived of that which you think is your right to claim in court. It is indeed the true Christian who can accept injustices for the sake of his Lord, as He suffered unjustly on our behalf.

LESSONS:

1. In regard to financial or material matters, one believer is not to go to court against another.
2. Believers who go to court are already defeated Christians.
3. Christ suffered unjustly on our behalf; we can suffer for Him.

1 Cor. 6:8 — *Being Defrauded Is Better Than Defrauding Another*

But you do wrong, and defraud, and that against your brethren!

It is preferable that the Christian suffer injustice rather than go to court against his brother, and it is not permissible for the suing believer to contend, in order to excuse his action, that his brother is not a true believer.

It is better for a Christian to have injustice done to him than to do injustice, and it is better to be defrauded than to defraud. These are explicit principles which the apostle Paul has laid down for believers.

In this verse, Paul states the real reason for the Corinthian Christians going to court: "But you yourselves do injustice and defraud, and you do this to your brothers!" The verbs are in the present active indicative (*adikeíte* [91], do injustice; and *apostereíte* [650], defraud), which means that you do this on a recurring basis, and you do it to your brothers. What an indictment upon the selfishness of the Corinthian Christians! When you see a tendency to litigation, you know it is motivated by selfishness. Paul sums it up in his hymn of love in 1 Corinthians 13:5: "Love does not seek its own."

LESSONS:

1. The most important thing in the life of a Christian believer is not possessions but relationships.
2. Relationships established by Christ are more precious than money. It is better to lose money than friends.
3. A fight over money among Christians will leave unbelievers with the impression that material things predominate in the lives of believers as is the case with themselves.
4. It is better for the Christian to lose possessions, and to suffer shame for the cause of Christ.

1 Cor. 6:9 | The Unrighteous Will Not Inherit God's Kingdom

Or do you not perceive that the unrighteous ones shall not inherit the kingdom of God? Be not deceived; neither fornicators, nor idolaters, nor adulterers, nor effeminate, nor homosexuals . . .

In verse 8, Paul warned against the practice of taking a brother to court over material things. The persons who live in this manner may be *ádikoi,* the plural of *ádikos* (94), unjust, but may not realize it. The interests of self should not overrule concerns for our brothers in Christ.

The Dangers of Unrighteous Behavior

Paul faces the problem by asking, "Or do you not perceive that the unrighteous ones will not inherit the kingdom of God?"

In the discussion regarding litigation which Christians were resorting to against other Christians before judges of the state, Paul calls the secular judges "unjust" or "unrighteous" (*ádikoi*) in verse 1, and "without faith" (*ápistoi* [571]) in verse 6. Both are designations of unbelievers. The secular judges are expected to be the administrators of justice, yet Scripture designates them as unjust. This is because their sense of justice is not of God, but it is a social justice (*díkē* [1349]) rather than a divine endowment resulting from faith and the new birth (Rom. 3:22). Not to harm another is to be righteous according to secular philosophy. In the teaching of Christ, that was the righteousness of the scribes and the Pharisees, but it was not sufficient to satisfy the righteousness of God (Matt. 5:20). Christ taught that we should go further and love our enemies (Matt. 5:43, 44). In the heathen mind, a just person (*díkaios* [1342]) was one who neither selfishly nor forgetfully transgressed the bounds fixed for him by the state. He gave to everyone his due, yet he still expected to receive what he conceived to be his right and would not in the least withdraw an assertion of his own claim. Christianity must continually combat such a view. The heathen, and by extension all unbelievers, say, My right is my duty. On the other hand, the Christian says, My duty is my right.

Now the duty of every Christian is love (1 Cor. 13). The Christians in Corinth had never really given up their worldly philosophy, and resorted to heathen judges to claim their rights against even their brethren. To obtain what may be legitimate by a way not permissible by divine precept is *adikía* (93), unrighteousness. Such a practice may show that we are unjust. We may get our legal rights, but be morally wrong.

Actions Speak Louder Than Words

The so-called believers in Corinth who practiced this type of behavior may not have been believers at all, the apostle Paul concludes. Although they may have been members of the local church, the love of God did not indwell them. In 1 John 3:10 John gives the difference between a child of God and a child of the devil. He says, "By this are evident the children of God and the children of the devil. Whoever does not practice righteousness in no way is of God, and he who does not love his brother." The question posed by Paul is, Do you really love your brother when you drag him before an unjust and unbelieving judge for material gain which you say is your right?

Don't forget that by engaging in such practices you show what you are, an unjust person as conceived by God, and as such don't you perceive that you cannot inherit the kingdom of God?

"Or do you in no [*ouk* {3756}, the absolute 'not'] way perceive [*oídate*, the perfect used as a present indicative of *eídō* {1492}, to perceive] that unjust people [*ádikoi*, unjust without the definite article which stresses any kind of injustice as described] shall not inherit the kingdom of God?" To claim one's right before unbelievers, and to claim it from a brother may classify such a person as unjust (*ádikos*). This is a serious departure from the teachings of Christ.

The Kingdom of God Can Only Be Inherited

"Unrighteous people [or unbelievers] shall not [*ou*, the absolute 'not'] inherit [*klēronomḗsousi*, the future indicative of *klēronoméō* {2816}, to inherit] *the* kingdom of God." The definite article "the" is not before the word "kingdom," meaning they will neither enter the kingdom of God nor receive the wonderful benefits of it which they would have had they truly believed and practiced the teaching of the Word of God.

In both verses 9 and 10 the verb that is used for participation in the kingdom of God is "inherit" (*klēronomḗsousi*). One inherits something for which he cannot work. Such is the kingdom of God as the rich young ruler learned when he asked the Lord, "Good Master [teacher], what good thing shall I do that I may inherit eternal life?" (Matt. 19:16; Mark 10:17; Luke 18:18). There was not anything he could do. The kingdom of God is gained only by inheritance, by grace. It is not an accomplishment. It is a gift which is bestowed only by receiving Jesus Christ by faith. When our Lord began His earthly ministry, both He and John the Baptist said, "Repent ye: for the kingdom of heaven [the same as the kingdom of God {Matt. 19:23, 24}] is at hand" (Matt. 3:2; 4:17; Acts 2:38).

The kingdom of God comes in two stages: first invisibly in the heart of the believer, and by and by it shall come visibly as a kingdom on earth (Luke 17:20, 21).

Our verse under study and also verse 10 refer to both comings of the kingdom, the present and the future—the invisible rule of Christ in the heart with the visible results in the lives of the sinners changing them to saints, and also the future kingdom when Jesus shall return to earth (Matt. 25:31; Rom. 8:10).

But why is the verb "inherit" used in the future tense? Because there is hope of salvation for every sinner if he repents and believes, but there is absolutely no way whereby he can inherit the kingdom of God if he continues in his sinful condition. Does the word "inherit" refer to receiving something after death? Under Jewish law this was so, but under Roman law, which was prevalent at the time of Paul's writing, it was being born into a family that gave one the right to become an heir, a possessor of all that belonged to the family. This also applied to adoption. Thus Paul in Romans 8:17 says, "If we are children, then we are heirs." We become children (*tékna* [5043], born children) by the new birth (John 3:1–13) through faith (Eph. 2:8, 9), for as many as receive Christ or believe on Him become God's children (*tékna*).

Heirs of God and Joint Heirs With Christ

By becoming children of God, we are placed in the family of God. The word "adoption" is *huiothesía* (5206) which comes from *huiós* (5207), son, and the verb *títhēmi* (5087), to place. The word "son" (*huiós*) is what Jesus is called, for He was the Son of God and the Son of man. But He was never called the child (*téknon*) of God, that is, born of God, but always the Son (*huiós*). Why is this so? Because He is God Himself (John 1:1, 14), not born of God. The word *huiós* is a step further in the relationship of Father and Son. It is not the relationship of an inferior to a superior, for Jesus spoke of equality in His eternal relationship with the Father: "I and the Father are One [*hén*, the neuter of *heís* {1520}, one in essence, not in personality]" (John 10:30). Christ was called *huiós*, Son, because voluntarily and by nature, He constantly conformed to the will and character of His Father.

We become heirs of God when we are born again, when we become children (*tékna*) of God (Rom. 8:17). We also become joint-heirs with Christ. The word for joint-heirs is *sugklēronómoi* (4789) from the preposition *sún* (4862), together, conjointly, and *klēronómoi* (2818), heirs. We as believers become partakers not only of the nature of God (2 Pet. 1:4), but also of all that is Christ's because of His voluntary participation in the Father's purposes and desires. That participation by Christ meant willingness to suffer in His incarnation. Inasmuch as we are willing to suffer with Him, we shall also be glorified with Him. This is the third statement in Romans 8:17. We prove our sonship (*huiótēs*) by our willingness to suffer with Christ as He suffered in the flesh for us. This suffering is demonstrated by presenting our bodies a living sacrifice pleasing unto God (Rom. 12:1). Paul sums it all up in Galatians 2:20 where he says, "I am crucified [*sunestaúrōmai*, which is the middle/passive of *sustauróō* {4957}, 'I have crucified myself'] with Christ: nevertheless I live; yet not I, but Christ lives in me: and the life which I now live **in the flesh**, I live by the faith of the Son of God, who loved me, and gave Himself for me."

In that we are born again by God and are children (*tékna*) of God, we lose the capacity to sin habitually (1 John 3:9, 10), and we thus inherit the kingdom of God. This is the spiritual kingdom of God. The Almighty becomes our ruler.

A Son of God Recognizes His Sin, Repents, Confesses, and Is Forgiven

As individuals we still have sin or the capacity to slip occasionally as did Paul who stated that sin indwelt him (Rom. 7:20). In the measure of our dedication to Christ, we are victorious (1 John 5:4, 5). Each time we have overcome, the victory will be acknowledged as we stand before the judgment seat of Christ "that we may be glorified together" (Rom. 8:17). The phrase "glorified together" is one word in the Greek— *sundoxasthṓmen*, the aorist passive of *sundoxázō* (4888), to glorify together, from *sún*, together with, conjointly, and *doxázō* (1392), to glorify, which is derived from *dokéō* (1380), to think, to recognize for what one is. Thus another inheritance we as born-again believers shall enjoy is that which we have allowed ourselves to be made by Christ.

True, in our Christian lives we may have presented our bodies to God who made them and, in the measure of our commitment to Him, we shall inherit the kingdom of God, which means the rewards of our commitment. It was this commitment and self-discipline that Paul had in mind when he wrote about himself to these same Corinthians: "But I keep under [*hupōpiázō* {5299}, to strike under the eyes, beat the face black and blue, give a black eye, mistreat, subject to hardship] my body and bring it into subjection [*doulagōgéō* {only in 1 Cor. 9:27 meaning to treat it as if it were a slave without a will of its own}]: lest that by any means when I have preached to others, I myself should be a castaway [*adókimos* {96}, not having passed the test and thus found unacceptable]." At the coming of Christ, the kingdom of God will not be the same for every believer, but will be commensurate to one's victories and works in this life (Rom. 14:10; 2 Cor. 5:10).

Those who grasp all they can of earthly possessions should consider the benefit of not only being ushered into the kingdom of God, but the future benefits of a holy, unselfish life (cf. Luke 22:29; 1 Cor. 15:50; Heb. 11:33; 12:28). Is it wise to lose so much for the temporary gain of so little?

Who Will Not Inherit the Kingdom of God?

"Do not be deceived [*mḗ* {3361}, the relative 'not'; *planásthe*, the present imperative of *planáō* {4105}, to deceive, go astray by not having a goal in life]." Paul warns not only about going to court against our brothers before unbelieving judges, but to be careful lest we fall into certain other practices that are even worse and which will totally exclude us from the kingdom of God. The selfishness demonstrated by legally seeking what is due to us may be an indication of deeper evils lurking within our hearts. Seeking self-satisfaction leads to the sinful lifestyles Paul describes. "Neither" (*oúte* [3777], neither, not even, which is made of the absolute *ou* and *te* [5037] which means "and" or "even") is followed by the practitioners of evil as follows:

Fornicators

The word "fornicators" (*pórnoi*, the plural of *pórnos* [4205], a male prostitute) is derived from the verbs *peráō*, to sell, and, in the New Testament, *pipráskō* (4097), to traffic, to sell. The Greeks considered one who prostituted himself for gain as a fornicator. Money is involved in prostitution as it is involved in litigation of a brother against a brother.

One can see a trend among the Corinthians. They were willing to go to court one against another. Although they were known as Christians, they were motivated by personal, material gain. Here, now, we have fornicators selling their bodies for gain. The trend is downward.

We are told in 1 Corinthians 5:9–11 not to keep company with fornicators. The Greek word for "keeping company" is *sunanamígnusthai*, the present infinitive middle form of *sunanamígnumi* (4874), to mix together. It comes from *sún*, meaning together, conjointly, and *anamígnumi*, to mix together, which is from *anā́* (303), on or upon, and *mígnumi* (3396), to mix, mingle. In this sentence, the compound verb means to mix or mingle together with the fornicators so as to give the idea that the Christian is one of them. In 1 Corinthians 5:11 we are advised not to mix (*sunanamígnusthai*) or join together with a so-called brother who is covetous *(pleonéktēs* [4123]) one who desires more for himself).

It is clear that the young man of whom Paul speaks in 1 Corinthians 5 was not a fornicator, although he fell into the sin of fornication. He does not call this man *pórnos*, but points out that *porneía* (4202), the sin of fornication, existed in the local congregation although as an exception.

The young man under discussion was a Christian who fell into sin, but he recovered as 2 Corinthians 2:5–11 indicates (see the author's book *Immorality in The Church—Can We Sweep It Under the Rug?*). Apparently he confessed his sin, as 1 John 1:9 says to do, and experienced that cleansing of the blood of Christ which cleanses us from **all** sin. This includes the sin of fornication, and enables us to be victorious over it (1 Cor. 6:11; 1 John 1:7; 2:1, 2).

As long as one continues in the sin of fornication, there is no possibility of inheriting the kingdom of God. Ephesians 5:5 says, "For this you know [*éste* {1510}, be; *ginṓskontes*, knowing, the present participle of *ginṓskō* {1097}, to experientially know] that no whoremonger [*pórnos,* fornicator] or unclean person, or covetous man who is an idolater [that is, who has made such sin his idol or god] has any inheritance in the kingdom of Christ and of God." Observe that again here as in 1 Corinthians 5:11 and 6:10, the fornicators are in the same group as the covetous, which shows that the motivation for resorting to secular courts was material gain. See also 1 Timothy 1:10; Hebrews 12:16; 13:4, 5.

Revelation 21:8; 22:15 tell us what will be the destiny of fornicators: "For . . . whoremongers [fornicators] . . . shall have their part in the lake which burns with fire and brimstone: which is the second death"; "For without are . . . whoremongers [fornicators]. . . ." It is to be noted that *pórnos* (fornicator) is the general name for anyone who sells his body sexually in any manner or form.

Worshipers of Idols

"Nor idolaters [*eidōlolátrai*, the plural of *eidōlolátrēs* {1496}, idol worshiper]." This occurs here in verse 9 and also in 1 Corinthians 5:10, 11 and 10:7. In Ephesians 5:5 and Colossians 3:5, the idol worshiper is equivalent to a covetous person. The idolater is a person who loves anything more than he loves God.

Those who worshiped mammon (*mammōnás* [3126], the god of money) were idolaters. Hence the covetous who have an insatiable appetite for money and material things are called idolaters. Idolatry (*eidōlolatreía* [1495]) was the sin among the heathen as contrasted with the Jews who worshiped Jehovah.

Adultery, a Form of Fornication

"Nor adulterers [*moichoí*, the plural of *moichós* {3432}]." This is a sin which also falls under the category of idolatry (Heb. 13:4).

Passive Homosexuals

"Nor effeminate [*malakoí* [3120], soft ones]." These are men who allow themselves to be used as if they were women, that is, passive homosexuals.

Active Homosexuals

"Nor homosexuals [*arsenokoítai* {733} from *ársēn* [730], male, and *koítē* [2845], a bed, meaning a man who lies in bed with another male]" (Rom. 1:27; 1 Tim. 1:10).

All these shall not inherit the kingdom of God. But they can be born again and become children of God and heirs (*klēronómoi*) of God (Rom. 8:17). However, they cannot be both sinners possessed of any of the above sins and at the same time heirs of God's kingdom.

<u>LESSONS</u>:

1. The scriptural perception of a righteous person is different than the perception of the philosophy of this age.
2. The kingdom of God is inherited, received by faith in Jesus Christ who died for our sins. One cannot work for it.
3. There is a present possession of the kingdom of God and a future enjoyment of the kingdom and its rewards.
4. All who engage in the sin of fornication, idolatry, adultery, effeminacy, and homosexuality cannot be possessors of the kingdom of God.

1 Cor. 6:10 | *Unrighteous Acts of Those Who Will Not Inherit God's Kingdom*

Nor thieves, nor covetous, nor drunkards, nor revilers, nor extortioners, shall inherit the kingdom of God.

In this verse, Paul continues the list of specific practitioners of sin who will not inherit God's Kingdom.

Covetous Persons

From covetousness springs the practice of going to court for material profit, elaborated in verses 1 through 8, and other sins enumerated here. The Majority Text has the covetous persons preceding the thieves. Therefore we shall examine covetousness first. A covetous person is the one who wants to have more than he already has. He fails to realize that no matter how much he manages to get, it will still not satisfy him. The Greek word is *pleonéktēs* (4123) from *pléon* or *pleíōn* (4119), more, and *échō* (2192), to have. It can mean a person who has an insatiable appetite for more, a person covetous of something that others have, a defrauder for gain.

A covetous person is also one who desires to have more than another. But why is that such a great sin? Why does that kind of covetousness deprive one from entrance into the kingdom of God? Because such a person, proving that he is selfish, puts himself in first place thus excluding God from being Master (Matt. 6:24).

A covetous person is not one who may be simply tempted to have some comfort which may characterize the life of another. He is rather one who is dissatisfied because he does not have more, or he does not have as much as another person. This is not merely an act of covetousness, but a ruling spirit of greed. When one possesses the kingdom of God, he is overwhelmed with the spirit of satisfaction that is derived from having God as his fulfillment. He possesses what the whole world cannot buy, because it is a spiritual quality of life.

The rich young ruler (Matt. 19:16–22; Mark 10:17–22; Luke 18:18–23) who came to Jesus had possessions in abundance. The Lord asked him to sell his possessions and give to the poor. This does not infer that when one sells what he has and gives to the poor, he can acquire eternal life. John 3:16 tells us that to have eternal life, one must believe on the Lord Jesus Christ. Christ was telling this young rich ruler that one who truly has eternal life would put his relationship with God first and paramount, and material things would be given a lesser position in this life.

The young man was unwilling to put material things second and spiritual qualities first. The Lord, on the other hand, urges us to put the spiritual first because He knows that nothing else can satisfy the spirit of man. One can possess the whole world and not possess peace and satisfaction.

To illustrate His command, "Take heed and beware of covetousness. For a man's life [*zōḗ* {2222}, the essence of life as contrasted with *bíos* {979}, the means of life, possessions] consists not in the abundance of the things which he possesses" (Luke 12:15), the Lord gave the parable of the successful farmer. This farmer's main concern was himself. He never thought of thanking God from whom comes every good and perfect gift

(James 1:17), and he never thought of his fellow man who needed him. He thus broke the two most important commandments delineated in Matthew 22:37–40, that is, to love God wholeheartedly and his neighbor as himself. Of him it was rightly said, "He laid up treasure for himself, but was not rich toward God" (Luke 12:21). He left Christ's question unanswered, "What is a man profited if he shall gain the whole world and lose his own soul? Or what shall a man give in exchange for his soul?" (Matt. 16:26).

The man, therefore, who is not willing to acknowledge the worthlessness of his material possessions in contrast to real life, that is, eternal life which can only come from faith in Jesus Christ, will not be willing to part with his possessions. The first thing that a blessed person (*makários* [3107], blessed) experiences is full satisfaction in possessing Christ, and he finds sufficiency (*autárkeia* [841]) in what he possesses, much or little. It is a question of which comes first, *zōḗ*, life, or *bíos*, the possessions of this earthly existence.

Let us not forget the words of Paul in 1 Corinthians 6:10 that "not even [*oúte* {3777}, nor, from the absolute negative *ou* {3756}, not; and *te* {5037}, and, even] covetous persons . . . shall inherit the kingdom of God." He who is not willing to place material things as less important than spiritual life, the greatest gift of all, eternal life, will not be given to him. That is why Christ said, "Seek ye first the kingdom of God, and His righteousness, and all these things [material things which will not detract from the value of the kingdom of God] shall be added unto you" (Matt. 6:33).

The so-called believer, a member of the Corinthian church but not necessarily a member of the body of Christ, who would sue his brother for material things would be a covetous person. He would rather have Christ shamed than have less of what could not make him "blessed" anyway. Material gain does not take first place for the true believer for whom to live is Christ and to die is gain (Phil. 1:21).

Thieves

In the Majority Text the thieves are listed after the covetous, and not before. This is logical. The act of stealing is the externalization of covetousness, desiring to have what another has, even if it must be by stealth. A covetous person is a thief in his heart until he finds the opportunity to externalize his inner desire.

Thieves here must be taken as those sinners who again place more trust in material things than in the spiritual gift of eternal life.

Judas was called a thief when he expressed his objection to Mary anointing the feet of Jesus with an expensive ointment (John 12:5, 6). He said she should, instead, have sold it so that the money could have been used to feed the poor. So also is the person who may defraud his brother by taking him to court.

Drunkards and the Kingdom of God

Who is a drunkard? Twice in the Epistles of Paul the word "drunkard" occurs. In 1 Corinthians 5:11 we read, "But now I have written unto you not to keep company if any man that is called a brother be a fornicator, or covetous, or an idolater, or a railer, or a **drunkard**, or an extortioner; with such a one, no, not to eat."

And again in 1 Corinthians 6:10 we find, "Nor thieves, nor covetous, nor **drunkards**, nor revilers, nor extortioners, shall inherit the kingdom of God."

The word in the Greek text is *méthusos* (3183), a person given to *méthē* (3178), drunkenness, which is from *methúō* (3184), to get drunk. A drunkard is a person who drinks wine or other substances to such excess that he loses his ability to make proper decisions. In Galatians 5:22, 23 in the catalogue of the fruit of the Spirit, the opposite of drunkenness is mentioned as temperance, which is *egkráteia* (1466), self-control. In the list of works of the flesh are listed *méthai*, the plural of *méthē*, drunkenness. In the KJV it is translated in the singular, "drunkenness." However, it makes no difference how a person willingly loses control of self or his or her rational capacity, that state of loss of control is a state of *méthē*, drunkenness or rational imbalance. The believer is to exercise self-control in all matters.

There are more intoxicating agents than wine that can make a person become drunk and lose his rational balance. Such are material elements that one takes by mouth or inhalations or injections which indirectly affect the function of the body. There are drugs of all kinds. There are also spiritual vices such as bad temper, hatred, resentment, jealousy, pride, or avarice that can make a person lose his or her rational balance, causing him to become drunk with anger or jealousy or such evils.

Drunkards are not capable of making a rational decision because they are in slavery to their lusts, and are unwilling to be enslaved to Christ. To have the kingdom of God is to have God as one's king. Since the drunkard is controlled by his passions and remains under their control, he will not have another to rule over him unless he experiences the new birth and is born into the kingdom of God. Man cannot have two masters (Matt. 6:24). It is impossible to be a drunkard, a man given to intoxicating drink or anything else that enslaves him, and at the same time have God as king. Upon receiving Christ and experiencing the new birth, the individual who is controlled by his or her passions ceases to be off-balance by anything worldly, be it physical or spiritual. That it is possible to change by having God as Master of one's life is demonstrated by what Paul says in verse 11: ". . . and these some of you **were**." This clearly states that the believer is no more what he used to be.

A Christian is a person who maintains a righteous proportion in all things. Commitment to Christ commands self-control in everything; in speech, in sleep, in work and recreation, in gain and ambition, not less than in food and drink. It condemns equally every form of excess: exaggeration in speech, extravagance in taste, outbursts of temper, inordinance of every form of appetite.

Let us not forget that this whole discussion of people who will not inherit the kingdom of God emanated from the prohibition of a Christian suing other Christians primarily over material things. If he does, he is drunk with the love of money.

Revilers

"Nor revilers . . . shall inherit the kingdom of God." Who are revilers? The word in Greek is *loídoroi*, the plural of *loídoros* (3060), a reviler, one who verbally abuses or berates. The word is of uncertain derivation. It is an adjectival noun which is found in the list of sinners who will not inherit the kingdom of God while they persist in their wrongdoing (Gal. 5:21).

Revilers represent sinners with whom Christians are advised in 1 Corinthians 5:11 by Paul not even to eat together, with the idea of having intimate fellowship. "But now I have written unto you not to keep company [*sunanamígnusthai*, the present middle infinitive of *sunanamígnumi* {4874}, to mix up together as if you were one of them], if any man that is called a brother [he is not a real brother] is a fornicator, or covetous, or an idolater, or railer [*loídoros*], or a drunkard, or an extortioner, with such a one, no, not to eat [*sunesthíein*, the present active infinitive of *sunesthíō* {4906}, to eat together as if you were one of them]." True Christians should not associate with a reviler, for he is likely to influence them for evil, while it is doubtful that the believer could influence him for good.

What does a reviler do? What is the poison with which he can destroy God's children? It is evil words. His tongue is his weapon. We are to avoid those who speak evil against others. When we find a conversation turning to gossip or criticism of others, we should not be drawn into it, and should make an effort to lift the conversation to a more spiritual level.

Consider, for instance, the blind man in John 9, whom Jesus healed. The veracity of the miracle was attested to by his parents who were, nevertheless, pressured by the Jews to deny that this miracle had been done by Jesus. The Jews said that the glory should be given to God, thus intimating that Jesus could not be God as He claimed. He was a sinner, they said (v. 24). The Pharisees then reviled the formerly blind man, saying to him, "You are His disciple; but we are Moses' disciples" (v. 28). And then they went on to say, "We know that God spoke to Moses: as for this fellow, we know not from where He is" (v. 29). "Reviled" (v. 28) meant defamed. They said that the fact that Jesus miraculously opened the blind man's eyes did not really matter, and they cast doubt on the deity of Jesus Christ and His claim that "he who has seen Me has seen the Father" (John 14:9).

In Acts 23:1–11 we find Paul accused of having reviled the high priest Ananias before the Sanhedrin because he responded to him with the words, "God shall smite you, you whited wall: for do you judge me after the Law, and command me to be smitten contrary to the Law?" (v. 3). The word that was used to accuse Paul was *loidoreís* (3058), you defame with words (v. 4). Paul's defense was that he did not know that Ananias was a high priest. So the verb *loidoréō*, to revile, means to speak evil of an established authority.

In 1 Corinthians 6:10 the adjectival noun *loídoroi*, revilers, is placed in company with thieves and extortioners as those who in no way will inherit the kingdom of God. Revilers are those who steal—not goods which the thieves do in stealth and extortioners do in plain daylight—but the reputation and the good name enjoyed by certain people. Many otherwise good people find it a great past time to spread all the gossip they hear about others. This is sinful.

Of our Lord, Peter said in 1 Peter 2:23, "Who, when He was reviled, reviled not again." This means that when Christ was demeaned, He did not reply back in the same manner, using the same techniques and insults. So a reviler is a person who with insults demeans another. He is a reviler when he insults the Lord's authority, and he cannot inherit the kingdom of God. This is a spirit of resistance against the conviction of the Holy Spirit in His witness as to who the Lord Jesus is (Matt. 12:31, 32; Mark 3:28–30; Luke 12:10). When a person speaks evil of Jesus Christ, he blasphemes against the Holy Spirit. In fact, the verb *loidoréō*, revile, has as its closest synonym the verb *blasphēméō* (987), to blaspheme, and *hubrízō* (5195), to insult, to use despitefully or shamefully. As with all the sinners enumerated in 1 Corinthians 6:9, 10, this one, the reviler, is a person of whom it must be stated that as long as he is a reviler, he cannot inherit God's kingdom.

You Cannot Practice Sin and at the Same Time Have the Kingdom of God

In Galatians 5:19–21 we have the works of the flesh, the actual sins which enslave people. The passage closes by saying that "they which do such things [*hoi prássontes*, the present participle of *prássō* {4238}, to practice, perform repeatedly or habitually, usually referring to what is bad] shall not inherit the kingdom of God." That this reviling or blaspheming against the Holy Spirit is something that can be repented from is indicated by 1 Corinthians 6:11 which says, "And these some of you were." This implies that these individuals had obtained forgiveness and admission into the kingdom of God, although they formerly were habitual sinners as those described in Galatians. Through repentance and the new birth, they were forgiven and became new creatures (1 Cor. 6:11).

The Believer's Attitude When He Is Reviled

What should our behavior as children of God be in this matter of being defamed or reviled by others? We are to imitate Christ "Who, when He was reviled, reviled not again" (1 Pet. 2:23). When we become the recipients of verbal attacks or insults, do we answer back with similar words? Remember that *loidoría* (3059), railing, is hurling destructive words at others. The Lord never did this according to 1 Peter 2:23 who recalled what Isaiah 53:7 prophesied in regard to His crucifixion: "He was oppressed, and He was afflicted, yet He opened not his mouth: He is brought as a lamb to the slaughter, and as a sheep before her shearers is dumb, so He opens not His mouth."

The apostle Paul in 1 Corinthians 4:12 says, "Being reviled, we bless." The word for "bless" is *eulogoúmen*, the present indicative of *eulogéō* (2127), to speak well of. Our words should be the opposite of reviling. Our reaction and endeavor in response to demeaning speech should be to speak well if humanly possible. If this is impossible, at least we can keep silent. The Holy Spirit that indwells us enables us to do so. We must act in such a way that the person will be convicted of his evil way, and cease and change. Our words become actions of benevolence.

The same thought is expressed in 1 Peter 3:9: "Not rendering evil for evil, or railing [*loidoría*, reviling] for railing, but contrariwise blessing [*eulogoúntes*, the present participle of *eulogéō*, to speak well of, bless] knowing that you are thereunto called that you should inherit a blessing."

Extortioners

In the same category with revilers are rapacious persons (*hárpages*, the plural of *hárpax* [727], an excessively greedy person, an extortioner). An extortioner is a person who by force takes what does not belong to him, and he does it with suddenness. A "snatcher" would be a good translation. These criminals rob unexpectedly in broad daylight by sheer superiority of force. Of course, they will not inherit God's kingdom, but it is encouraging to know that some who were extortioners are not now, having received the kingdom of God. The kingdom of God is the satisfying substitute for sin of all kinds. This passage shows that no sinner is beyond the grace of God to change through Jesus Christ.

LESSONS:

1. Through inheritance from Adam, man has rejected God and adopted a bankrupt lifestyle that is not satisfying (Rom. 5:12).
2. Sin, or the desire of the flesh, is a state that cannot satisfy, no matter how many external works of the flesh the sinner may attempt in an effort to expiate (Gal. 5:16–21).
3. The Holy Spirit supernaturally must be allowed to work out the miracle of regeneration (John 3:1–13) to bring about the change in the human personality (Eph. 2:1, 2, 8–10), so that instead of the works of the flesh, there will be the "work" of the Spirit (Gal. 5:22–25). Then will come full satisfaction, not from the satiety of sin, but from the work of grace in the human heart.
4. There is no sinful practice from which the Holy Spirit cannot liberate man. To show this in practicality, the apostle Paul is saying in effect: Such and such was at one time a fornicator, an idolater, an adulterer, a thief, a drunkard, a reviler, an extortioner, but he is no more. The explanation of the change is the grace of God in Christ, the substitution of the kingdom of God in the human heart.

1 Cor. 6:11 | *What Christians Were, What They Are Now, and Why*

And such some of you were; but you washed yourselves, but you have been sanctified, but you have been justified in the name of the Lord Jesus, and by the Spirit of our God.

Paul has enumerated what believers cannot be—fornicators, idolaters, adulterers, effeminate, homosexuals, covetous, thieves, drunkards, revilers, extortioners—and at the same time claim to have entered God's kingdom. He then affirms how some of the believers in Corinth had been sinners living such a sinful lifetyle. They had been any or all of these things. In other words, they were unrighteous (*ádikoi* [94]) and unbelievers (*ápistoi* [571], without faith) even as the judges to whom they resorted to solve their disputes. In such disputes, there can be no equitable solution, or any solution at all, that will correspond to the righteousness and faith of the Lord Jesus Christ. All of the sinners whom Paul enumerated wanted tangible material things or pleasures. Why should someone struggle to acquire more and more since no amount of anything is ever enough to satisfy? It is necessary to substitute the desire for material earthly things with the only One who can truly and fully satisfy.

Think What You Were!

If you had been a judge in your previous state, Paul reasons, could you have rendered faithful and spiritual solutions to the problems among believers? If not, why do you now go to such people knowing that they are not spiritual? Secular judges are possessed of a philosophy such as some of you had in your previous sinful state, and they cannot understand the state of grace. They cannot comprehend how a Christian can live in the world, but not be of the world. There is a basic difference between the actions of a child of God and a child of the devil (1 John 3:10). Thus Paul explains his reasoning.

Why Some and Not All?

Why does Paul say that only **some** of you were such, and not **all** of you, since "all have sinned, and come short of the glory of God" (Rom. 3:23)? Again, in Ephesians 2:3, we find Paul saying, "Among whom also we all [he includes himself] had our conversation [behavior] in times past in the lusts of our flesh, fulfilling the desires of the flesh and of the mind; and were by nature the children of wrath, even as others."

In 1 Corinthians 6:9, 10, Paul gives the symptoms of unrighteousness and unbelief, and it is only a partial, although typical, list. Another list is found as "the works of the flesh" in Galatians 5:19–21. Observe carefully verse 21 which says, ". . . and such like: of the which I tell you before, as I have also told you in time past, that they which do such things shall not inherit the kingdom of God." The symptoms of unrighteousness and unbelief are never given in one complete list, nor are the gifts (*charísmata*, the plural of *chárisma* [5486], the result of grace [*cháris* {5485}]) of God (1 Cor. 1:4, 5; 12:4–11). Of an unrighteous unbeliever, any evil or all of them put together can be expected. Why? Because unredeemed self is in the center. But why does a brother sue a brother before unbelievers? Because he would rather defend the interests of self in disregard to what this will do to the name of Christ. Selfishness is the core of every other external sin quoted in verses 9 and 10.

"Such" Refers to Lifestyles Lived Prior to Salvation

This is why Paul does not say *toioútoi* (5108), such, referring to people, but *taúta* (5023), these things, these sins by which you were characterized. This indicates that an unjust person, an unbeliever, is capable of any or all of the symptoms of unrighteousness or unbelief. This is the nature of fallen man.

Cleansing and the Element of Cleansing

"But you are washed [*apeloúsasthe*, the aorist middle of *apoloúō* {628}, to wash away, from *apó* {575}, indicating completeness, and *loúō* {3068}, to wash, bathe]." Actually, *apoloúomai* means to wash oneself clean, and the middle aorist, *apeloúsasthe*, means that you washed yourselves clean. The passive would have been *apeloústhēte*, you were washed. Furthermore, the two verbs that follow are definitely aorist passives, *hēgiásthēte*, "you were sanctified," which is the aorist passive of *hagiázō* (37), to sanctify, make holy; and *edikaiṓthēte*, "you were made righteous," which is the aorist passive of *dikaióō* (1344), to render just, make righteous.

So what we have is the first verb in the middle voice, "you washed yourselves clean [*apeloúsasthe*]," while the other two verbs are in the passive voice, "you were sanctified [*hēgiásthēte*], and you were justified [*edikaiṓthēte*]." The last two activities that lead to sanctification and to justification are accomplished by Someone other than oneself. They are works accomplished by the triune God—the Father, Jesus Christ, and the Holy Spirit. But if it were only the will of God involved, He would sanctify and justify all human beings. First Timothy 2:4 says: ". . . who [Jesus Christ] will have all men to be saved, and to come unto the knowledge of the truth." It is God's wish for all men to be saved. Second Peter 3:9 states that God is "not willing that any should perish, but that all should come to repentance."

Why, then, does God not do what He wants? We see that man's salvation involves repentance, and not all men are willing to repent and believe. Therefore, not all men are saved. John 3:16 states, "For God so loved the world, that He gave His only begotten Son, that **whoever believes** in Him should not perish, but have everlasting life." While salvation is offered to all, it is received by some but rejected by others (John 1:12). Man's will enters into the picture. This is why *apeloúsasthe*, "you washed yourselves," is in the aorist middle. *Apoloúō* refers to the availability and element of cleansing and refers to man's willingness to go where it is found to wash himself. This is equivalent to the exercise of repentance and faith, both of which are absolutely necessary for salvation (Matt. 3:2; 4:17). Man must avail himself of the element of cleansing. God will not force it upon an unwilling subject.

Now what is the element of cleansing? Actually it is through the blood of Christ shed on the cross that we have our cleansing. First John 1:7 states explicitly that "the blood of Jesus Christ His Son cleanses us from all sin." Actually, having shed His atoning blood, it is Christ who cleanses: "If we confess our sins [the confession which involves repentance], He is faithful and just to forgive us our sins, and to cleanse us from all unrighteousness."

Not Mere Water, but Calling Upon the Name of the Lord

Could this possibly refer to the water of baptism as the agent of cleansing? The verb *apoloúō* is used also in Acts 22:16 in connection with Ananias' instruction to Paul: "And now why do you tarry? Arise, and be baptized, and wash away [*apólousai*] your sins, calling [*epikalesámenos*, having called upon, which is the aorist participle middle of *epikaléō* {1941} derived from *epí* {1909}, upon, and *kaléō* {2564}, to call] on the name of the Lord." The translation is not quite explicit enough. The verb that is translated "calling" is *epikalesámenos*, having called upon, which is the aorist participle of *epikaléomai*, to call upon. What was it that washed away the sins of Paul, the baptism by Ananias or his calling upon the name of the Lord? Certainly it was the calling upon the name of the Lord as Peter asserted explicitly on the day of Pentecost: "And it shall come to pass, that whoever shall call [*epikalésētai*, should call upon, the third person aorist subjunctive of *epikaléomai*, call upon] on the name of the Lord shall be saved" (Acts 2:21).

The same promise from the prophet Joel (2:32) was recalled by Paul himself in Romans 10:13: "For whoever shall call upon [*epikalésētai*] the name of the Lord shall be saved." And then in verse 14, he asks the question, "How then shall they call on [*epikalésontai*] Him in whom they have not believed?" So a person who believes will call upon the name of the Lord. Paul was saved having called on the name of the Lord and was consequently called upon by Ananias to be baptized. Note that he was saved first and then baptized (Acts 10:44–48).

What Does "the Washing of Water by the Word" Mean?

Let us consider Ephesians 5:26 which says, "That he might sanctify and cleanse it with the washing of water by the word." The question to ask is, whom does Paul refer to by the word "it"? In Greek this is *autḗn*, her, that is, the church, having cleansed it (*katharísas*, the aorist participle of *katharízō* [2511], to cleanse) with the washing (*loutrṓ*, the dative of *loutrón* [3067]) of water by the word (*en* [1722], in, by; *rhḗmati* [4487], utterance), meaning the doctrines and promises of God revealed and taught in the Bible (see John 3:34; 8:47; 17:8; Acts 10:37; Rom. 10:17;

Eph. 6:17; 1 Pet. 1:25). What is this washing or bath (*loutrón*) of the water by the word? It is clearly the Word of God which acts like washing with water in its cleansing ability.

A father was admonishing his young son to read the Bible daily. "I can't understand what it is saying," said the boy. "You see that basket on the porch in which you carry the coal for the furnace? Go down to the stream and bring it back full of water," said the father. The boy did as he was instructed, but after a few attempts, came to his father saying, "I tried, Dad, but the water just runs through the basket. I can't get anything." "That is the way it is with the Word of God, son," said his father. "You may not think you are getting anything. But your heart and mind are like that basket. If you notice now, the basket is clean inside."

The word "baptism" (*báptisma* [908]) occurs only in Ephesians 4:5 where it states: "One Lord, one faith, one baptism." Does that refer to water or Spirit baptism? Undoubtedly it speaks of the Spirit baptism. That there is such a baptism, we refer to explicit statements of the Word of God as in Matthew 3:11; Mark 1:8; Luke 3:16; John 1:33; Acts 1:5; 10:44–48; 11:16; 1 Corinthians 12:13. The oneness of the baptism of the Holy Spirit is to be contrasted with water baptism by a variety of people such as Paul by Ananias, and other believers by other servants of Christ. Paul, speaking concerning water baptism, asks in 1 Corinthians 1:13–17: "Is Christ divided? Was Paul crucified for you? Or were you baptized in the name of Paul? I thank God that I baptized none of you, but Crispus and Gaius; lest any should say that I had baptized in my own name. And I baptized also the household of Stephanas: besides, I know not whether I baptized any other. For Christ sent me not to baptize, but to preach the gospel: not with wisdom of words, lest the cross of Christ should be made of none effect."

In 1 Corinthians 6:11, water baptism is not mentioned at all, and the verb *apeloúsasthe*, you washed yourself clean, cannot refer to water baptism because water has cleansing value when applied to the body, but not to the soul or spirit. No exclusively external deed will lead to an inner change. Washing ("baptizing" in Luke 11:38) of the hands does not cleanse one's spirit and soul. Each one of us needs the Spirit baptism for that.

Are Those Who Are Not Baptized Lost?

Water baptism is an outward confirmation of that inner cleansing that is accomplished by the Spirit of God because of the shed blood of the Lord Jesus Christ. The Word of God explicitly states that those who do not believe are judged already (John 3:18). It does not say that those who are not baptized are judged.

But what is the meaning of 1 Peter 3:21 which says, "The like figure whereunto [even] baptism does also now save us (not the putting away of the filth of the flesh, but the answer of a good conscience toward God,) by the resurrection of Jesus Christ"? (see note on 1 Pet. 3:21 in the *Hebrew-Greek Key Study Bible*). The word to observe is *antítupon* (499), antitype or figure. Think of what water baptism symbolizes—our death together with Christ and our rising again in His resurrection (Rom. 6:4–11), and this is what takes place with the person who believes on the Lord Jesus. It is the act of faith itself which is symbolized by water baptism that saves a man. This is not merely the putting away of bodily filth; it is much more than that. It is the cleansing of the life of the believer. It is an attestation (*eperṓtēma* [1906]) of a benevolent conscience (*suneídēsis* [4893], from *sún* [4862], conjointly together, and *eídō* [1492], to know intuitively as a result of one's relationship with God). *Suneídēsis* is to agree with God. But in order for man to be in agreement with God, it takes the resurrection of Jesus Christ. It is what water baptism symbolizes—faith in the crucifixion and resurrection of Christ—that brings the life of God in man, not simply water baptism.

Only faith can cleanse a fornicator, an adulterer, an idolater, an effeminate, a homosexual, a greedy person, a thief, a drunkard, a reviler, an extortioner. If it were ever possible to cleanse such sinners by water baptism, it would be so easy, and it would have not necessitated the coming of Jesus Christ into the world to suffer and die for us.

Sanctification Is the Work of God

Paul then says, "but you were sanctified." By whom? By God. The verb *hēgiásthēte* is the aorist passive of *hagiázō*, which means to render clean in a moral sense. In a graphic manner, Paul describes people who lived an immoral life. These went to the fountain of life, which is the cross; they washed themselves clean, and God saw the sincerity of their faith and confirmed the miracle of His purification of their lives.

Paul, in writing to believers, those who were made holy in their lives, uses the term *hēgiasménois*, the perfect participle of *hagiázō*, to make holy. In 1 Corinthians 1:2 Paul writes "to them that are sanctified [*hēgiasménois*, the dative plural passive participle] in Christ Jesus, called *to be* saints, with all that in every place call upon the name of Jesus Christ our Lord, both theirs and ours." It is to be noted that immediately following the word "sanctified" is the expression "in Christ Jesus." The saints are separated from sin, and they are placed as saints "in Christ Jesus." The value of deliverance from sin is not merely the freedom we have from it, but the attachment to Jesus Christ. It does not say "in Jesus" but in "Christ Jesus." The divine name of the Lord Jesus comes first.

The Lord is never called "Christ Jesus" except after His resurrection. We find this first in Acts 19:4, and thereafter in Romans 3:24; 8:2; 15:5; 1 Corinthians 1:2, 30; Galatians 3:26; 4:14; Philippians 2:5; 3:3, 8; Colossians 1:4 and Hebrews 3:1 (TR), as well as in a number of other verses.

Our Lord prayed for His own: "Sanctify them through your truth: Your word is truth" (John 17:17). And in verse 19, we have, "And for their sakes I sanctify Myself, that they also may be sanctified through the truth." The NIV renders the Greek better: "that they too may be truly sanctified [*hēgiasménoi en alētheía*, sanctified in truth or truly]."

That the three Persons of the Triune God participate in that sanctification is made clear by these statements:

God the Father is the sanctifier: "And the very God of peace sanctify you wholly; and [I pray God] your whole spirit and soul and body be preserved blameless unto the coming of our Lord Jesus Christ" (1 Thess. 5:23).

The Lord Jesus is also the sanctifier: "To them that are sanctified in Christ Jesus" (1 Cor. 1:2). "In the name of the Lord Jesus" in 1 Corinthians 6:11 applies not only to the verb, "you were justified," but also to "you were sanctified" (see also Heb. 13:12).

The Holy Spirit is the sanctifier as our verse declares: "and by the Spirit of our God."

Justified Before the Father

Following repentance and salvation, the former sinner is justified: "You were justified [*edikaiṓthēte*, the aorist passive of *dikaióō* (1344), to justify; see the discussion in *The Complete Word Study Dictionary: New Testament*, pp. 462–67]." This implies that as sinners we stood guilty before God, but we were released from our guilt because of the work of Jesus Christ which we accepted as we believed. The justice of God the Father has been fully satisfied through the blood of Christ shed on our behalf. Just think what standing we have with God! We can approach Him at any time (Rom. 5:1, 2).

LESSONS:

1. Being of a depraved nature, we were slaves to sin from which the grace of God freed us. This does not mean that we cannot fall into an act of sin (Rom. 7:20; 1 John 1:9; 2:1, 2) of which we would become painfully aware, but, nevertheless, for which we may ask and receive forgiveness.
2. One cannot have within him the kingdom of God and at the same time keep practicing a sinful lifestyle with its evil manifestations.
3. The source of cleansing is the blood of Christ (1 John 1:7). It takes an act of faith to take the blood and apply it to our own hearts (Rom. 10:8–13) and to be washed from sin. No material thing such as the water of baptism can wash away our sins. We sin because we are sinful, but we do not become sinful because we sin.
4. Our slavery to our sinful nature is removed through the appropriation of the blood of Christ. That shedding of blood satisfied the justice of God. He receives us as if we had never sinned. That is what being "justified" by Him (Rom. 5:1) means.
5. Our hearts are washed which means that our justification is not academic. It is practical in that it affects our daily lives. This is our sanctification. It makes us holy as He is holy. We no more practice sin. We become freed from the slavery of sin, and we become slaves of righteousness and God (Rom. 6:18, 22; Gal. 4:3). If sanctification is not the result of the washing of our sins and justification by God, then we are under the mere delusion of having been washed and justified.
6. It takes the work of Christ and of the Holy Spirit for the accomplishment of our washing, justification, and sanctification.

1 Cor. 6:12 | *All Things Are Permissible, but Not Necessarily Good*

All things are permissible for me, but all things are not expedient: all things are permissible for me, but I will not be brought under the authority of any.

These words constitute a principle of Christian behavior. The apostle Paul arrived at this principle from the temptation faced by members of the Corinthian church when they encountered differences concerning material possessions. Evidently, church members were taking one another to court to have their disagreements resolved by an unjust and unbelieving judge.

While this is something that worldly people frequently do, is it right for a Christian brother to exercise such action against a brother? In other words, does a believer have the right to do as a Christian what he has a right to do as a citizen?

What Regulates Christian Conduct?

It has well been stated that man has rights, but the Christian has duties. It is not what one may do but what one should do.

The standards by which a Christian judges his actions are different than the standards of the world. When worldly people are due something from a fellow human being, they demand to be paid. The apostle Paul, in stark contrast to the unbeliever, says to his brethren in Corinth: "Why do you not rather take wrong? Why do you not rather *suffer yourselves* to be defrauded?" (1 Cor. 6:7). And then in verses 9 to 11, he reminds some of the Corinthians that they were once the worst possible sinners, but that they have been cleansed. They were sanctified and justified in the name of the Lord Jesus and by the Spirit of the Lord. In the twelfth verse, he tells them that they have a duty to consider not only what is good for themselves, but whether it is good for the cause of Christ and for others. It may be a personal right which, for the sake of Jesus Christ and for the sake of others, may be given up rather than demanded. This cannot be regulated; it is a matter of personal conviction. What is necessary more than regulation is the training of what Paul calls "conscience" (1 Cor. 8:7).

The Freedom That Is in Christ

The unbeliever is a slave of sin. Paul says in Romans 6:17, ". . . you were the servants [*doúloi* {1401}, slaves] of sin." The moment, however, one becomes a believer and is born again, he becomes a slave of Christ (Rom. 1:1; 6:18, 22; 2 Cor. 4:5). In the exercise of slavery to Christ, however, there is more freedom practiced than can be imagined, and thus Paul says in Galatians 5:1, "Stand fast, therefore, in the liberty wherewith Christ has made us free, and be not entangled again with the yoke of bondage."

This slavery to Christ, however, is different from other slavery. It is a slavery that comes with the privilege of sonship. Thus Paul says in Galatians 4:7, "Wherefore you are no more a servant [*doúlos*, slave], but a son [*huiós* {5207}]; and if a son, then an heir of God through Christ." So before our salvation we were slaves (*doúloi*) of sin and were under the authority of sin. After our salvation, although we are called the slaves of Christ, we enter into the family of God and are actually sons. Being sons (*huioi*) means choosing to do that which a son would do. We obey Christ because we love Him and we want to please Him.

Christ promised us not slavery, but freedom. He gives us His nature (2 Pet. 1:4), and we experience freedom from the bondage of sin and are thus enabled to realize the ideal of human nature created in the image of God (Rom. 6:20ff.). This freedom we had lost because of our fall in Adam (Rom. 5:12). The freedom of the Christian will lies not in the power to do whatever we please, but in the power to choose and follow that for which God created us in the beginning. God Himself is absolutely free, precisely because He is absolutely perfect. Christ's power to make others free springs from His own divine freedom—that model oneness with the Father wherein He did always the things that were pleasing to Him (John 8:29). In Christ's gospel, freedom after His own pattern is offered to all. It comes from union with Christ, for apart from Him we can do nothing (John 15:5). This is the freedom to do that which pleases the One who makes us free, and it is the Son who can make us free, and we become free indeed (John 8:36). The doctrine of the indwelling of Christ through the Holy Spirit (Rom. 8:9, 10; 2 Cor. 6:16), and the consequent endowment of His disciples with freedom and power, was taught according to the fourth gospel by Jesus Himself (John 15:14–17). It is constantly enforced by Paul as the testimony of his own experience. Apart from the law of the Spirit of life in Christ Jesus, the will is powerless to realize its own ideals (Rom. 7:19ff.; 8:2ff.). But in accepting Christ as our Master and by yielding to His will as supreme, we pass into "the glorious liberty of the children of God" (Rom. 8:21). It is this freedom with which Paul was possessed, and he could thus say, "All things are permissible to me."

The Freedom of Sonship

We can only understand the slavery of the New Testament in the context of the Greek world. A slave had no freedom to choose. If he was given freedom, he was made a son, and was adopted into the family of his master. This is why Paul, in Romans 8:15 says, "For you have not received the spirit of bondage again to fear; but you have received the Spirit of adoption [*huiothesía* {5206}], whereby we cry, Abba, Father." And in Galatians 4:5 he writes: ". . . to redeem them that were under the law, that we might receive the adoption of sons." To move from slavery to sonship meant to be given the life of liberty. Adoption was one recognized way of giving freedom to a slave. There is thus no inconsistency, but only a striking paradox, when this experience which is described as freedom is also described as servitude to God (cf. 1 Pet. 2:16; Rom. 6:22). Thus true freedom consists in the desire to obey God as Father.

What Are "All Things"?

When Paul says, "All things are permissible to me," he was speaking as a son (*huiós*) of God, and, of course, he was not referring to all evil things. This is indicated by verse 18 which picks up one of the sins enumerated in verses 9 and 10, namely fornication. He says, "Flee fornication." None of the sins enumerated here and elsewhere as "the fruit of the flesh" (Gal. 5:19–21) are among the "all things" which are permissible.

Also, this passage of 1 Corinthians 6 should be read as a whole, for we read in verses 9 and 10 that fornicators, idolaters, adulterers, effeminate, homosexuals, greedy, thieves, drunkards, revilers, and extortioners will not inherit the kingdom of God. This ought to provide the context of verse 12 under discussion that "all things are lawful unto me." Certainly those things which do not permit a person to enter the kingdom of

God could not be considered permissible, nor could Paul be accused of practicing any of them.

It is the privilege of the Christian believer to make his own choices, but his difficulty lies in making those choices in view of their eternal consequences. He must choose between the good things of life and the excellent things, having eternity in view. This is not always easy.

Lot's Choice

Wealth can be both a blessing and a curse. What gave rise to this discussion which the apostle Paul had with the Corinthians was also a matter of their possessions (vv. 3, 4) and the right of the individual.

A very good illustration of this is the choice that Lot had to make between the place where he would dwell and that which should be his Uncle Abraham's dwelling place. There arose a dispute between his servants and Abraham's servants, and the dispute was how to divide up the land to support their increasing cattle. Abraham said to Lot in Gen. 13:7–10:

> Let there be no strife, I pray you, between me and you, and between my herdsmen and your herdsmen; for we are brethren. Is not the whole land before you? Separate yourself I pray you, from me: [if you will take] the left hand, then I will go to the right; or if [you depart] to the right hand, then I will go to the left. And Lot lifted up his eyes, and beheld all the plain of Jordan, that it [was] well watered everywhere, before the Lord destroyed Sodom and Gomorrah, [even] as the garden of the Lord, like the land of Egypt as you come unto Zoar.

We are so limited by looking at things as they are at the time and not at what they might develop to be. We can see the apparent, but not the potential (cf. 2 Cor. 4:17, 18).

Then we read that Lot made his choice. It was a selfish choice that did not deprive him of God's righteousness within him, but it was not the best choice he could have made. "Then

Lot chose him all the plain of Jordan; and Lot journeyed east: and they separated themselves the one from the other. Abraham dwelt in the land of Canaan, and Lot dwelt in the cities of the plain, and pitched [his] tent toward Sodom" (Gen. 13:11, 12). He chose to go where the grass was greener, but the greener side is not always the best side.

Lot chose the city of Sodom where the people were exceedingly wicked before the Lord (Gen. 13:13). Their material prosperity was attractive, so attractive that it blinded Lot's moral judgment. First, Lot was attracted by the riches of Sodom and Gomorrah; then we find that he entered. Evidently he became quite comfortable living in the midst of its sin, for we find him sitting at the gate as a ruler over Sodom and Gomorrah (Gen. 19:1).

Lot dwelt in the city, but Abraham dwelt in a tent (Gen. 13:18). Materially, the city was to be preferred. Outwardly Lot succeeded, but his success became a curse. Almost all his family died as a result of Lot's greedy and sinful choice, and his two daughters who did live fell into terrible sin, and the consequences are still being felt to this day (Gen. 19:30–38).

The choice which Lot made was not in itself so sinful that it excluded him from the kingdom of God. In 2 Peter 2:7, 8 he is referred to as "just and righteous Lot." It also says, "He was vexed with the filthy conduct of the wicked. For that righteous man dwelling among them, seeing and hearing, vexed his righteous soul from day to day with their unlawful deeds." Lot made his choice, but he could not choose the consequences of his choice. Little did Lot imagine that the consequence of his selfishness would lead his two daughters to commit incest with him.

Liberty to Choose, But . . .

Certainly Paul is speaking about the liberties that we have in Christ. This is what we call the *adiáphora*, the matters that are nonessential. These are discussed in this epistle and elsewhere as being food, drink, holy days, circumcision, and so on. Such matters perplex the Christian. There are things for which we do not have specific rules or regulations in Scripture. It is up to the conscience of the Christian to judge. Such choices do not involve our eternal salvation, but our eternal reward. They are choices between that which is good and that which is excellent, and each has its reward. Paul is addressing the prudent exercise of our Christian liberty.

Guidelines for Choosing What We May or May Not Do

Observe that Paul says, "All things are permissible to **me**." He uses the Greek word "to me" (*moí*). This is the dative singular of *egṓ* (1473), I. While he speaks about himself individually, every other Christian must make his own choices. Being in Christ, we have perimeters of choice that we must personally make and for which we bear responsibility as to its consequences. We make the choices, but God sets the consequences.

The verb *éxestin* (1832) which is used in the phrase, "All things are permissible to me," is the impersonal form of *éxeimi* (1826) which is derived from the preposition *ek* (1537), out of, and *eimí* (1510), to be. It means "it is possible," referring to the mere possibility of propriety, that is, it is lawful, right; it is permitted or within my power. This is called *exousía* (1849), freedom within boundaries.

In Matthew 20:1–16 we have Jesus' unique parable of the workers who were dispatched to the vineyard. The first group was hired to work for a specific time and for a specific salary. For twelve hours' work they were to be paid one *dinar* (*dēnárion* [1220], a monetary unit). However, there were several other workers who were recruited during the day; some at nine o'clock in the morning, some at noon, some at three o'clock, and some at five o'clock with six o'clock being closing time. To all those who were hired after the first group, the employer did not promise a specific reward. He just told them that he was going to give them a just reward (Matt. 20:4, 7). They agreed and went to the vineyard because there was a need to be met. They did not know what their reward would be, but they trusted the employer. When paytime came, the master decided to first pay those who worked one hour only. To the surprise of everybody, for one hour's work he gave a whole *dinar* which was the reward promised to those who worked twelve hours. The contractual workers immediately expected that they would receive more. However, when they received only that to which they had agreed, they protested and called the employer unjust. The employer in his answer gave a very pointed reply in verse 15: "Is it not permissible [*éxestin*, lawful, permissible] for me to do what I will with my own? Is your eye evil, because I am good?" It is as if the employer were saying to them, You accepted having the promise of a certain reward for a certain task, while the group that belonged to the second category of workers had no promise of exact pay. My sense of justice was the only promise.

Such are the choices which a believer makes. They are not to be based on the glitter of gold, but on the certainty of the justice of God. Paul preferred not to choose what was immediately rewarding and convenient, but what he saw as eternally rewarding, based on God's justice. He chose the less comfortable life and was even willing to suffer and die if necessary for the cause of Christ. Although he defends the right to receive a salary for his work for the Lord, he chose not to (1 Cor. 9:1–18). He defends the right, however, of those who do receive a salary. For that extra mile he decided to walk in his Christian service, which he calls work "without charge" in verse 18, he is to receive a special reward. These are the things that a person is permitted to choose that are not sinful in themselves, but they have special rewards. Each of us has choices to make that are personal, and they affect not only us but also others and the work of God.

Don't Make a Law Out of Your Personal Preferences

In the example of Lot, we saw how our decisions affect us personally in the long run. It is wrong, however, to take the choice which the apostle Paul made for himself and apply it to others as a mandatory obligation they must follow. This is why we prefer to translate *éxestin* as "it is permissible" instead of "it is lawful." Paul's choice to work without being paid cannot be imposed on all gospel workers, nor is celibacy to become a law of acceptable service for the Lord just because Paul chose that lifestyle. Such an imposition is legalism which the Scriptures condemn just as sin is condemned. Paul handles this problem in Colossians 2:20 where he writes: "Wherefore if you be dead with Christ from the rudiments [*stoicheíōn*, the plural of *stoicheíon* {4747}, element, essential component of life] of the world, why, as though living in the world, are you subject to ordinances?" The word translated "subject to ordinances" is the verb *dogmatízesthe,* you dogmatize or make dogmas out of personal choices. *Dogmatízō* (1379) is derived from *dógma* (1378), decree, ordinance, and it is as if Paul were saying, Why do you make your personal choices dogmas or rules to be followed?

The legalizers say, "Touch not; taste not; handle not" (Col. 2:21). These dogmas are all to perish with the using, for they are "the commandments [*entálmata*, the plural of *éntalma* {1778}, human precept in contrast to *entolḗ* {1785}, God's commandment] and doctrines [*didaskalías,* the plural of *didaskalía* {1319}, teaching] of men" (Col. 2:21, 22). Paul is arguing that a choice of life for oneself ought not to become a teaching or commandment imposed upon others.

Is What I Choose Not Merely Permissible, but Helpful?

Paul mentions this phrase, "All things are permissible to me," not only here in 1 Corinthians 6:12, but also in 1 Corinthians 10:23. Of the whole quotation which was occasioned by certain foods considered unclean, Paul says, "All things are permissible for me, but all things are not expedient: all things are permissible for me, but all things edify not. Let no man seek his own, but every man another's [wealth]. Whatsoever is sold in the shambles, [that] eat, asking no question for conscience sake: for the earth is the Lord's, and the fullness thereof" (1 Cor. 10:23–26). This concerns food that is available for the believer to eat and enjoy. If, however, one has an objection to eating certain foods for certain reasons, he should not insist that others refrain also, making this a dogma. Each person must answer for his own conscience and not impose his views on others.

Self Discipline Is Beneficial

Self discipline is good. Paul says in 1 Corinthians 9:27, "I keep under [*hupōpiázō* {5299}, to strike under the eye, beat the face black and blue, give a black eye] my body [observe **my** body, not somebody else's body], lest **I myself** should be a castaway [*adókimos* {96}, unacceptable, unapproved, unworthy, spurious)." Paul is stressing that his personal discipline was entirely a private matter and could not be imposed upon others. He was free to choose, to enjoy the earth and all its fullness, but he did not choose satiety. He submitted himself to many kinds of bodily sacrifices, one of which was not to marry. Paul chose to be a man of few wants. He determined to not do anything that would in any way render his life less productive in the service of his Lord.

Pluck and Eat Corn When You Are Hungry

Consider the example of the Lord Jesus. The first time that the impersonal verb *éxestin* is used in the New Testament is in Matthew 12:2. The Pharisees saw the disciples of Christ as they were walking through the field on the Sabbath. They were hungry and plucked the ears of corn and ate them. "But when the Pharisees saw it, they said unto Him, 'Behold, Your disciples do that which is not permissible [*éxestin*] to do upon the Sabbath day.' " The Lord Jesus told the Pharisees that it was not wrong to pluck the corn on the Sabbath day in order to satisfy one's hunger. He was asserting what Paul later taught, that "the earth is the Lord's, and the fullness thereof" (1 Cor. 10:26). We are free from legalism and the slavery of tradition.

Healing on the Sabbath

The second time that the verb *éxestin,* "is permissible," is used is in Matthew 12:10. On the occasion that the Lord healed the man with the withered hand, He was asked, " 'Is it lawful to heal on the Sabbath day?' that they might accuse Him." The answer of the Lord was most significant. He said to them that they would rescue their sheep if it fell into a pit. They did not do this out of mercy for the sheep, but because it concerned an item of value to them.

The Lord did not deliberately encourage the profaning of the Sabbath, but if the choice had to be made between feeding oneself of available food and going hungry on the Sabbath, they should make a choice according to their conscience. If the choice presented itself to them to help somebody, even if it were on the Sabbath, they should do it. To deny a needy person of help was a greater evil. It is this choice between the good and the better that confronted the disciples and which we are frequently called upon to make in our daily living.

Suffer Minor Loss to Total Destruction

We find the same principle also taught in the Sermon on the Mount. The Lord said in Matthew 5:29, "And if your right eye offend you, pluck it out, and cast [it] from you: for it is profitable for you that one of your members should perish, and not [that] your whole body should be cast into hell." And then in verse 30, He says, "And if your right hand offend you, cut if [off], and cast [it] from you: for it is profitable for you that one of your members should perish, and not [that] your whole body should be cast into hell." Now, there is nothing wrong with the right eye and the right hand. God has made both the eye and the hand and has made them well. But if that which brings one pleasure from beauty—the eye—or gives one the pleasure of touch—the hand—causes the whole body to be tempted instead of being blessed, then it is better to limit our freedom of enjoyment. It is the freedom and its voluntary limitations by the Christian that Jesus Christ and Paul are addressing.

Consider Our Brothers

Not only for our own sakes must we limit our freedom, but for the sake of others. Paul says, "but not [*ou* {3756}, the absolute 'not'] all things are expedient." The word translated "expedient" is *sumphérei* the third person singular of *sumphérō* (4851) which is made up from the preposition *sún* (4862), conjointly together, and *phérō* (5342), to bring. It means to be profitable, advantageous, to contribute or bring together for the benefit of another. Paul is telling us here that man does not live unto himself alone and does not die unto himself (Rom. 14:7). Consciously or unconsciously, our lives affect others. When it is necessary to make a personal choice, we should ask not only how it is going to affect ourselves, but also others. Is it going to be harmful to them, or is it going to be profitable? In 1 Corinthians 8:7–13 Paul discusses this extensively. Suppose, says Paul, that a Christian was invited by a nonbelieving friend or co-worker to a dinner at his home. It was a common practice in those days to go to the temple or the market-place to buy the meat of the animals that were sacrificed to idols. What should a Christian do in such a case? Should he eat that meat and run the risk of being accused of having fellowship with idols? It was a perplexing problem facing the Christians then, even as there are many problems today that must be decided by conscience and Christian principles. Paul's advice was that we should go to the dinner and eat what is put before us and be thankful for it. Remember the general principle that "the earth is the Lord's and the fullness thereof," and that settles the matter as far as each person is concerned.

However, the situation now becomes more complex. Perhaps there is sitting near you one who is a weaker brother. His conscience would be bothered if he knew that the meat was from the temple. Our choice should be influenced by the consideration of that brother and how he would view our action. There is no sin in the action itself, but there will be sin if we show no concern for the conscience of another.

How far is the believer's liberty in Christ, which he has received from Him, to go? In such a case, Paul instructs us, he is to consider how the exercise of his freedom is going to affect his brother. If his brother would in any way be tempted to compromise and have fellowship with idolatry, it is better not to eat the meat sacrificed to idols. It is better to sacrifice one's personal freedom than to tempt a weaker brother.

This is important for us to consider in the matter of drinking intoxicating beverages, for instance. If it were not for their intoxicating aspects, there would be no problem. This varies from person to person, of course, but no one can drink unlimited amounts of alcoholic beverages and remain unaffected. I am a teetotaler. The reason, however, is not that such beverages can make me drunk, nor that legalists forbid it. Rather it is lest I should offend my weak brother that I do not drink. If the enjoyment of my freedom could possibly cause problems for anyone else, I would prefer to give up my freedom. It is more excellent to consider the weakness of my brother than the enjoyment of anything in life. Unfortunately, there is no lack of weak brothers in the Christian church (Rom. 14:1), and, if God is our Father, we should consider our brother with as much love for him as we have for ourselves.

Freedom to Choose

Of utmost importance are the words of Paul in Romans 12:2: "And be not conformed [*suschēmatízesthe*, the present imperative of *suschēmatízō* {4964}, to conform outwardly which is derived from *sún*, together, conjointly with, and *schēmatízō*, to conform to the scheme of things or to the outward appearance of things, take the shape of] to this world." Paul is urging believers not to outwardly appear as doing what the world is doing, but to be "transformed [*metamorphoústhe*, the plural imperative middle of *metamorphóō* {3339}, to change in substance] by the renewing of your mind, that you may prove what is that good, and acceptable, and perfect will of God. For I say, through the grace given unto me, to every man that is among you, not to think [of himself] more highly than he ought to think; to think soberly [*sōphroneín*, the present infinitive of *sōphronéō* {4993}, to exercise the faculty of a sober or saved mind, to acknowledge that there are limitations to one's own liberty], according as God hath dealt to every man the measure of faith" (Rom. 12:3). The Greeks realized that freedom can go too far and that man has been given the ability to limit his freedom. They called this faculty to have a sober mind *sōphroneín*. *Sōphronéō*, to limit one's freedom, applies to the believer especially. We are to place limitations on our freedom when, if not exercised, it may lead to the destruction of our fellow believer or of any other human being including ourselves.

Personal Interests Above the Interests of the Gospel

The Corinthian believers who were suing their fellow believers thought that the result of their actions was a private matter, but it was not. There is no action absolutely private. Although possibly they may have attained their personal rights in securing the possessions which they thought belonged to them, how would this affect the cause of Christ? How would this influence the reputation of the local church of which they had the privilege of being a part? "All things are not expedient," not only to self, not only to others, but also to the cause of Christ. Would we ever want to use the freedom that Christ gives us to hurt Him and His church? Or to put it positively, shall we use the wealth and health that the Lord has given us to accomplish the most for Him, or shall we use them primarily for ourselves and give Him the crumbs, so to speak (Luke 16:21)?

The Limits Imposed by a Sound Mind

In 1 Corinthians 9 the apostle Paul writes, "Am I not an apostle? Am I not free?" Even an apostle might exercise his freedom in apostleship in demonstration of his power. In some churches, leaders may assume that they have absolute authority, perhaps even infallibility, as some had whom Paul calls superapostles (*huperlían*, derived from *hupér* [5228], super, and *lían* [3029], much) in 2 Corinthians 11:5; 12:11.

In 1 Corinthians 9:4 Paul says, "Have we not authority [*exousía*, power, which is derived from *éxestin*, it is permissible] to eat and to drink?" Yes indeed, but Paul also had a *sōphrosúnē* (4997), a sound or saved mind to guide his faith.

The apostle Paul in writing to Titus also gives a piece of advice that is necessary for all Christians: "For the grace of God that brings salvation has appeared to all men, teaching us that, denying ungodliness and worldly lusts, we should live soberly [*sōphrónōs* {4996}, wisely making judgments with a sound mind], righteously, and godly, in this present world" (Titus 2:11, 12). Two things stand out in these verses, the denial of worldly lusts and soberness of life in that which is permissible.

Was Jesus Obligated to Pay Taxes?

One of the perplexing situations in which the Christian is found in this world is what he should do in regard to paying taxes which support things with which he does not agree. In reality, he has no choice. This question was asked of Jesus. "Tell us, therefore, what you think. Is it permissible [*éxestin*] to give tribute unto Caesar, or not?" The Lord's answer was the paragon of perfection: " 'Whose is this inscription and image?' They said to Him 'Caesar's.' Then said He to them, 'Render therefore unto Caesar the things which are Caesar's . . .' " (Matt. 22:17, 20, 21).

There is another incident in the life of Christ that only Matthew, a former tax collector, records. It concerns the perplexing question as to who must pay the temple taxes which were obligatory for the Jews.

> And when they were come to Capernaum, they that received tribute money [taxes] came to Peter and said, "Does not your Master pay tribute?" He said, "Yes," and when he was come into the house, Jesus prevented him [was the first to speak to him] saying, "What do you think, Simon? Of whom do the kings of the earth take custom or tribute? Of their own children or of strangers?" Peter said to Him, "Of strangers." Jesus said to him, "Then are the children free" (Matt. 17:24–26).

The Lord Jesus was indicating that He was free, since the temple was His Father's house. He could claim exemption as a right, and so could His disciples since they were strangers in this world and, as such, they were exempt (Heb. 11:13). However, the Lord said that although we are strangers in the world, we should still pay taxes. While we are not of the world, yet we live in the world and should obey man-made rules as long as they do not fundamentally undermine our fidelity to God.

Observe the reason the Lord gave for paying taxes. In verse 27 He said, "Notwithstanding, lest we should offend [*skandalísōmen* {4624}, scandalize] them, you go to the sea, and cast a hook, and take up the fish that first comes up; and when you have opened his mouth, you will find a piece of money: that take, and give unto them for Me and you." The Lord exercised here His liberty of Sonship. He also used His omniscience and His omnipotence in the exercise of "all authority" which He had received from the Father on His incarnation as the God-Man (Matt. 28:18). He placed a limitation on His liberty in that although He did not actually have to pay taxes as God on earth, nor did Peter as His disciple, yet He chose to do so. As G. H. Morrison writes,

> But then had Jesus insisted on His rights, is it not easy to see what would have happened? Jesus saw in an instant what would happen. He had proclaimed the sanctity of law; now men would say He was a lawbreaker. He had urged obedience to Moses' representatives; now He was openly defying them. And so, not with His eyes upon His own, but with His eyes on the unbelieving world, the tax was paid lest they should be offended.

In other words, Christ limited His liberty in the supreme interest of the gospel. He deliberately abdicated His rights when asserting them might have been a stumbling block. He was come to seek and save the lost, and though the lost might hate Him and revile Him, He would do nothing, although permissible, that might make it more difficult to win them.

When Choosing What to Do, Think of Unbelievers Who Are Observing

The Christian must also consider how exercising his freedom will affect others.

> All we are taught is that in our use of freedom we must remember those who are without, and how by what we allow ourselves in Christ, they are likely to be affected toward the gospel. If the kind of life that we are living makes it less easy to believe in Christ; if our behavior, whether at work or play, is silently hardening anybody's heart, then, though everything we do is justified and well within the boundaries of our liberties, in the eyes of Jesus there is something wrong. All things are permissible, but all are not expedient, sometimes in the interests of our safety. All things are permissible, but all are not expedient, sometimes in the interests of our brother. All things are permissible, but all are not expedient, because around us there is a Christless world and men with their poor, blind eyes are judging Christ by what they see in His professing people. (From a chapter entitled "The Limits of Liberty" by G. H. Morrison in *More Meditations on the New Testament and Psalms*, AMG Publishers, pp. 144–50.)

We Must Consider What Effect Our Choices Will Have on Us

In this verse, the apostle Paul twice says, "All things are permissible to me." In choosing that which is permissible, however, there is one caution to be observed. At the beginning of the tasting of something that is good, we must ascertain whether it is habit forming and whether it could possibly take possession of us and control our appetites. "But I will not [*ouk*, the absolute 'not'] be mastered by anything." What I have translated "be mastered" is the word *exousiasthḗsomai*, the future passive of the verb *exousiázō* [1850], to control, to exercise authority upon, be under the power of. The verb is related to *exousía*, authority, liberty, right.

Often we have seen medications which are good for a person's illness, but the label carries the warning "Habit Forming." There are things in this life which are available and lawful, but caution should be exercised lest they become habit forming, and once the habit is formed, it is difficult, if not impossible, to overcome it. The time to avoid this is at the beginning and not at the end when it is too late.

The first time the verb *exousiázō* is found is in Luke 22:25, and the circumstance of its use is very interesting. The disciples were overcome with the desire to be preeminent in the kingdom of God that Jesus was going to establish. In answer to their request, the Lord said, "The kings of the Gentiles exercise lordship [*kurieúousin,* the present indicative of *kurieúō* {2961}, to rule, have dominion over, lord over] over them; and they that exercise authority [*exousiázontes*, the present active participle of *exousiázō*] upon them are called benefactors." Here the kings are presented as those who, upon becoming lords or rulers, exercise absolute authority, and yet they demand the title of "benefactors." That is typical of anybody or anything that becomes the ruler of our lives. As our benefactor, at first it seems good and we desire it. Little by little, however, as it gains control and masters us completely, it is too late to free ourselves. Today, we are demanding more and more benefits from our government, but the more we get, the more control our "benefactors" exercise. We must remember that anything or anybody that is big enough to give us what we want is also big enough to control us. In Genesis 47:13–26 we read that in a time of famine, the Egyptians demanded food from Joseph. He became their benefactor, but in the end they became Pharaoh's slaves (vv. 20, 23, 25). A tyrant may, to start with, come in the guise of a benefactor and wants to be considered as such, but he may end up being a tyrant, which is true of things also.

Authority Within Marriage

Besides 1 Corinthians 6:12, the only other occurrence of the verb "exercise authority over" is in 1 Corinthians 7:4 in relation to marital authority. "The wife has not power [*exousiázei*] over her own body, but the husband: and likewise also the husband has not power [*exousiázei*] over his own body, but the wife." This is the authority that is given in marriage in that the wife's body becomes available to her husband, and vice versa. This authority is exclusive within marriage. However, in 1 Corinthians 7:3 we are admonished to show "due benevolence" (TR, KJV), that is, to respect the well-being of the spouse.

Is It Expedient?

First Corinthians 6:12 teaches us to be alert regarding any pleasure. Is it expedient? Is it good for me, for others, and the glory of God? Is it habit forming, and can it possibly enslave me?

Of paramount consideration is that we do not cause harm to anybody nor the cause of Christ in the exercise of the personal liberty we have gained in Christ Jesus. Paul holds his liberty as a cherished possession. He boasts of being a bond slave of Jesus Christ, but he will be in bondage to no other master, human or habit. Remember Christ died to make us free from sin, not free to sin. Surely, then, we are not going to allow ourselves to be brought into bondage to any mere habit or pleasure.

A Safe Guide to Fellowship or Participation

First Corinthians 10:23 says, "All things are permissible for me [*éxestin*], but all things are not expedient [*sumphérei*]. All things are permissible for me, but all things edify not [*oikodomeí*, the present indicative of *oikodoméō* {3618}, to build, to edify]." The question, then, which one should ask him or herself is not whether there is any harm in what he does, but whether there is any good. Does it help to build up character? Shall I be the better for it or shall I be enslaved? Is it too much to demand that man, the crown of God's creation, should be served only by the things that edify and ennoble? Surely we are too highly prized by God to allow ourselves to be injured by any passing gratification. The cost is far too high. Let us remember that our characters, the quality of our innermost selves, matter eternally. Christ came to earth and became like us in order that He might make us like Himself. Life provides the opportunity of growing to be like Christ and thus fitting ourselves for that abode which He has gone to prepare for us.

This does not mean that life becomes narrow and joyless, for Jesus enjoyed life to the full. One of His last wishes was that His joy might be shared by His followers. A Christlike life can be full of real and lasting joy, accepting all things as from God who gives us all things richly to enjoy. The deepest joy is found in the presence of the Lord for at His right hand there are pleasures forever more (Ps. 16:11; 1 Cor. 6:13).

LESSONS:

1. It is permissible for the Christian to choose, but he must consider carefully the consequences of his choices upon himself, upon others, and upon the cause of Christ.
2. When we are free from the bondage of sin, we are free to live the ideal human life for which God created us.
3. The believer must choose not only between good and evil, but between the good and the excellent.
4. Many choices a person must make do not involve his eternal salvation, but his eternal reward.
5. We should not try to force our own personal choices on others as rules to follow.
6. To deny a needy person of help on the Lord's day is wrong.
7. We are to limit our freedom if it harms our fellow man.
8. We should obey the laws of the land as long as they do not undermine our fidelity to God.
9. Many things which appear as being beneficial to us frequently end up tyrannizing us.

10. The paramount question to ask oneself is not “Will this harm me, others, or the cause of Christ?” but, rather, “Will it edify me, others, and advance the cause of Christ?” (1 Cor. 10:23).

1 Cor. 6:13 — *How Free Are We?*

Foods for the belly, and the belly for foods: but God shall do away with both it and them. Now the body is not for fornication, but for the Lord; and the Lord for the body.

Of fundamental consideration is how far a man can go in the exercise of his freedom. While a man may determine the extent of his individual freedom, his will is determined by his character. We are confronted with alternative choices, but we must understand we are bound by a divine design.

What Food and How Much Shall I Eat?

Food is necessary for the sustenance of life, a product of the earth which God has provided. It is in the midst of Paul's discussion in 1 Corinthians 10:23–33 concerning things which are permissible that he twice quotes Psalm 24:1, "The earth is the Lord's and the fullness thereof." It is true that even in the abundance and variety of food God has provided that man is challenged by Paul who says, "All things are permissible to me, but not all things are expedient" (1 Cor. 6:12; 10:23). Even in the realm of eating, a Christian must exercise his freedom of choice as discussed by the apostle Paul in Romans 14. The Christian is free to choose his food and the quantity of it, but he is to be guided by whether his choice will offend his weaker brother or harm the gospel or his body in any way. In Romans 14:17 Paul says, "For the kingdom of God is not meat and drink; but righteousness and peace, and joy in the Holy Ghost." Here in 1 Corinthians 6:13 he says, "Meats [*brṓmata*, foods, the plural of *brṓma* {1033}, food which stresses the variety of food] for the belly and the belly for foods." In other words, the apostle Paul is stressing here that abstinence from or eating certain food does not determine one's entrance into the kingdom of God, for it all ends up in the belly. As we must exercise judgment and restraint in what we eat and the quanity we consume, so in life we must exercise judgment as to what we must flee from and also restraint in what we do.

In our consideration of food and the belly, as believers we must remember that these refer only to our earthly life. "But God shall destroy [*katargḗsei*, the future indicative of *katargéō* {2673}, to render inoperative] both it [the stomach] and them [foods]." Therefore they should never be given preference or preeminence in our lives.

The Body of Jesus Christ

We can discern a little concerning the future constitution of our bodies through the examination of the body of the risen Christ. We must observe it in relation to what it was prior to His resurrection and then compare it to what it was capable of doing after His resurrection.

First, when the Word of God speaks of the body (*sṓma* [4893]), it means the living body as such and, in particular, the body of a living person (Matt. 6:22; 26:12; Mark 5:29). The word for a dead body is entirely different. It is *ptṓma* (4430), a lifeless body, a corpse. Occasionally, however, the word "body" (*sṓma*) is used for a corpse (*ptṓma*) as in Matthew 27:52, 58, 59 and Luke 17:37, but this is rare. Jesus acknowledges the real rights of our corporeal body as it exists today. He was neither an ascetic nor a preacher of asceticism, for, as He said, "The Son of Man came eating and drinking" (Matt. 11:18, 19). At the same time, we find Him teaching a clear recognition of a duality in human nature as did the apostle Paul. Both Christ and Paul taught that a distinction is drawn between body (*sṓma*) and soul (*psuchḗ* [5590], the immaterial part of living man) and flesh (*sárx* [4561], the material part of the personality) and spirit (*pneúma* [4151], the immaterial part of the personality). The soul is that part in man which animates him inasfar as consciousness of his environment is concerned, and the spirit is that which distinctively makes man conscious of God. In Matthew 6:25 Jesus said, "Therefore I say unto you, take no thought [*mḗ* {3361}, the relative 'not'; *merimnáte*, the present imperative of *merimnáō* {3309}, to be anxious, to worry to the degree of affecting one's balance] for your life [*psuchḗ*, soul, representing the body as united with the soul] what you shall eat, or what you shall drink; nor yet for your body [the function of the living body], what you shall put on. Is not the life [*psuchḗ*] more than meat [*trophḗ* {5160}, (food)], and the body [*sṓma*] than raiment?"

In Matthew 26:41 our Lord draws the distinction between the flesh and the spirit: "Watch and pray, that you enter not into temptation: the spirit [*pneúma*] indeed is willing, but the flesh [*sárx*, the living body] is weak." The Lord lays strong ties between the immaterial and the material. Though the body is a true part of our humanity, its value is not to be compared for a moment with that of the spirit (Matt. 10:28). The body of Jesus before His resurrection, like our body, was a natural (*psuchikós* [5591]) body. It was living flesh. That is why Jesus experienced hunger (Matt. 4:2), was wearied with journeying (John 4:6), suffered pain (Matt. 27:26), and finally underwent death. His death, however, was not because of any sin of His own, but because of our sin (Heb. 4:15), for He died for our sins (1 Cor. 15:3).

Jesus' body after death was delivered by Pilate to Joseph of Arimathea who wrapped it in a clean linen cloth and laid it in his own new tomb (Matt. 27:58–66.) where it remained until the moment of His resurrection. His body did not see corruption (Acts 2:27). In Acts 2:31, His body is designated as His flesh (*sárx*) which is the purely live material part of His personality when the Spirit is separated from it. Ours, however, experiences corruption (*diaphthorá* [1312]) when the separation of the spirit from the living flesh occurs.

Our Body at Death

At death our body loses its God-given ability to consume food. Paul expressed it correctly in saying that "God shall destroy both it [*koilía* {2836}, stomach, belly] and them [*brṓmata*, foods]." This is a direct act of God. It is as if the apostle Paul is rebuking believers for their divisions over foods because they considered them of paramount importance. We make our belly such an important part of our life, but it is only temporary and of minor significance. The temporary is not to be compared in value with the heavenly. Food, although necessary, is for this earthly life as is the belly since we are going to have a heavenly body consequent to our resurrection. The heavenly body is going to be different than our present earthly body, but it is still going to be an individual body bearing correspondence to our earthly body.

Accountability of Our Earthly Life

It is important what we allow our body to do in this life, for we shall give an account in our future life how we behaved in our present bodies: "For we must all appear before the judgment seat of Christ; that every one may receive the things done **in his body**, according to what he has done, whether it be good or bad" (2 Cor. 5:10).

In Romans 14:6–13 there is a discussion about food: "For one believes that he may eat all things; another, who is weak, eats herbs. Let not him who eats despise him who eats not; and let not him who eats not judge him that eats: for God has received him" (vv. 2, 3). And then in verse 10 Paul asks the question, "But why do you judge your brother? Or why do you set at nought your brother? For we shall all stand before the judgment seat of Christ."

It is evident that we are all going to be judged as to how we cared for our earthly bodies, and the consequences of that are going to bear on our future body. Therefore, this is a serious matter, and it behooves us to be careful.

Termination of the Present Functions of Our Earthly Bodies

"But God shall destroy [*katargḗsei*] both it and them." In the resurrection the Lord is going to render inactive both food and the belly. The word which is translated "destroy" (*katargḗsei*) comes from the preposition *katá* (2596), an intensive meaning down, against, and the verb *argéō* (691), to be idle. It really means to cease to be active, to be idled. They will not have to adhere to the functions for which they were originally made.

We shall not need to eat to sustain our resurrection body as we do now. Such things, therefore, which divide the believers now are not worthy of Christian disunity because of their temporary nature. Paul says in Colossians 2:16, "Let no man, therefore, judge you in meat or in drink." In John 6:27 our Lord said, "Labor not for the meat which perishes, but for that meat which endures unto everlasting life." As we do not desire to be judged for the food we eat, so we must not judge others as to their convictions.

The Function of the Belly in Relation to Food Will Not Always Be the Same

Paul wants us to recognize what our natural body now is on earth and what it will be when it is resurrected. This he describes in 1 Corinthians 15:42–49. The contrast is between the earthly body which is corruptible and the heavenly body which is incorruptible. As Jesus had to eat when He was in the flesh, so do we, but we would be wise to follow His guidelines to consider what influence we bring upon others and upon the cause of Christ. Our conduct in the body will affect our future spiritual body (2 Cor. 5:10).

The Word of God does not reveal that our body shall be destroyed in the sense of its ceasing to exist. Nor does it say that we are going to be a human being without a body. The body is going to be preserved, but the Lord is going to refashion it. The word that the apostle Paul used in Philippians 3:21 to describe this radical change is *metaschēmatísei*, the future of the verb *metashēmatízō* (3345), reshape, made up of the preposition *metá* (3326), denoting change of condition at a later stage, and the verb *schēmatízō*, to shape, form. Although this basic verb is not found in the New Testament, the noun *schēma* (4976), scheme or outward shape, is. It is found in two places: 1 Corinthians 7:31 and Philippians 2:8. The relationship that exists between food and the stomach will somehow be affected. The belly will not be the only way whereby food is going to be enjoyed, and foods are not going to be the only means for the nourishment of the body. The body which the Lord is going to give us at His coming and at the resurrection of the believers will be differently constituted and the sustenance of its members maintained differently. That we will eat in the resurrection seems to be quite definite for our Lord ate after His resurrection, and God has promised us the wedding feast of the Lamb.

The Body Is to Be Kept Pure

In stark contrast to the function of food for the body stands the body itself. "But [*dé* {1161}] the body is not for fornication." The *dé* should be translated "but."

The verb "is not" is implied indicating that this is an eternal truth without chronological limitation. At no time did God create the body for fornication, which in the New Testament is presented as a gross and hideous sin. God created the sexual act to be practiced only within marriage. The word "not" in this verse is expressed with the absolute negative *ou* (3756). Immorality is not a matter left to our judgment or to our conscience as is food. It is strictly forbidden.

The Greek word for "fornication" is *porneía* (4202) which is any sexual sin, any deviation from the divine order, and is forbidden to the Christian in the exercise of his freedom. In verse 18, Paul emphasizes, "Flee fornication." An example of fornication is that of Tamar sitting on the roadside to entice Judah (Gen. 38:12–26). Such action was subject to the death penalty (Gen. 38:24; Lev. 21:9; Deut. 22:21). Fornication includes being unfaithful to a marriage oath (Judg. 19:2).

Fornication is viewed by the apostle Paul as so evil that we are commanded to absolutely abstain from it. The word that he uses in 1 Thessalonians 4:3 is *apéchomai* (567), to abstain. Under no circumstances is fornication permissible (Acts 15:20, cf. Rom. 1:29).

One cannot be a believer and be a practicing fornicator. Scripture is adamant about this: "Know you not that the unrighteous shall not inherit the kingdom of God? Be not deceived: neither fornicators, nor idolaters, nor adulterers, nor effeminate [passive homosexuals], nor abusers of themselves with mankind [homosexuals], nor thieves, nor covetous, nor drunkards, nor revilers, nor extortioners, shall inherit the kingdom of God" (1 Cor. 6:9, 10).

Sexual Activity Is Not a Necessity as Is Eating

Paul, in the context of 1 Corinthians 6:12–20, says that fornication is not to be considered a necessity as is food. While the nutritive system of man belongs to the perishing system of this world, the body is the organ of the spirit and the temple of the Holy Spirit, bought by Christ for His own service. To unite it to a harlot or any immoral person is an act of sacrilege, of self-violation, and it breaks the union between Christ and the believer. It is a sin to be repented from, for it breaks our fellowship with God (1 John 1:9; 2:1, 2).

The Choice Is Ours

We are presented with a choice: we can either give ourselves to fornication or to the Lord. When one is given to the Lord, he cannot be given to fornication. Romans 6:6 speaks of the work of the Lord in our lives: "Knowing this [*ginṓskontes* {1097}, to experientially know] that our old man is crucified." The verb "is crucified" is *sunestaurṓthē*, the aorist passive indicative of *sustauróō* (4957) derived from *sún* (4862), conjointly together with, and *stauróō* (4717), to crucify. Christ took upon Himself our old self with its body of sin and crucified it on the cross with Himself. The exact translation should be "was crucified." Why was our old self crucified? That the body of sin may be made inactive (*katargēthḗ*, the aorist passive subjunctive of *katargéō*, rendered inoperative). What is the result of that? "That henceforth we should not serve sin." The Greek is *mēkéti* (3371), no more, made up of the relative "not" (*mḗ*), and *éti* (2089), anymore. This stands in contrast to *oukéti* (3765), absolutely not anymore, from *ou*, the absolute "not," and *éti*, anymore. But while the old man was crucified together with Christ, the saved man is still not sinless. Satan still tempts him and sin still dwells in his body (Rom. 7:20), but he does not sin habitually. The verb for "serve sin" is *douleúein*, the present infinitive of *douleúō* (1398), to serve as a slave, thus meaning to compulsively serve sin.

"But for the Lord; and the Lord for the body." Paul's view of the body as an essential part of the human personality is clearly stated here. It is not for fornication nor for sin, but for the Lord. To develop bodily wholeness is the duty of a Christian. In Corinth the perverted notion had grown that since the body was not a part of the true personality, bodily acts were morally indifferent things. That is why Paul says in 1 Thessalonians 5:23, ". . . and the very God of peace sanctify you wholly, and I pray God your whole spirit and soul and body be preserved blameless unto the coming of our Lord Jesus Christ." And in Romans 12:1 he says, "I beseech you therefore, brethren, by the mercies of God, that you present your bodies a living sacrifice, holy, acceptable unto God, which is your reasonable service." In 1 Corinthians 6:19 he says, "What! know you not that your body is the temple of the Holy Ghost which is in you, which you have of God, and you are not your own?" Paul fervently defends that the body of a Christian belongs to the Lord and is a member of Christ Himself and a sanctuary of the Holy Ghost. He makes every member of the body expressive of the indwelling of Christ who permeates not only the body, but every manifestation of it. Yet his view of the communion of the body in man's spiritual life and its participation in the sanctifying powers of the divine Spirit did not blind Paul to the fact that the body, as we know it, is weak and tainted, ever ready to become the instrument of temptation and an occasion of stumbling (Rom. 6:19; 1 Cor. 9:27). So Paul, side by side with the truth that the body is a divine sanctuary, sets the demand that sin should not be allowed to reign in our mortal bodies, that we should obey it in the lusts thereof (Rom. 6:12).

The Human Body and the Spiritual Body

Thus on the one hand we have an overwhelming sense of the worth of the body in a human personality, and on the other, a clear recognition of its present limitations and unfitness in its earthly form to be a perfect spiritual instrument. The proof of the first is seen in Paul's attitude toward the bodily resurrection. To him the resurrection of Christ was a fact of the most absolute certainty (Rom. 1:4; 1 Cor. 15:3ff.). That fact carried with it the assurance that the dead are raised (1 Cor. 15:15ff.). Had he thought of the body as something essentially evil, and if he had not been persuaded of its absolute worth, his hopes for the future life would have centered in a bare doctrine of the immortality of the soul. But while Paul was passionately convinced of the resurrection, he did not believe in the resurrection of the present body of flesh and blood (1 Cor. 15:15). He looked for a body in which corruption had given place to incorruption (1 Cor. 15:42, 43), and humiliation had been changed into glory (Phil. 3:21). His doctrine of the resurrection includes the assurance that when the dead in Christ are raised (he has little to say regarding others), it will not be in the old bodies of their earthly experience. It will be in new bodies adapted to heavenly conditions (1 Cor. 15:47–54), bodies that are no longer merely physical; that is, moving on the plane of man's natural experience in the world. They will be spiritual bodies redeemed from every taint of evil and fitted to be the worthy and adequate organs of a spiritual and heavenly life (1 Cor. 15:44–49).

The believer realizes he was crucified with Christ and thus belongs to the Lord. This, however, does not mean an effortless attachment to the Lord. Galatians 2:20 says, "I have crucified myself with Christ." The Greek verb is *sunestaúrōmai* which is the perfect middle/passive indicative of *sustauróō*, to crucify with. This verb has the middle meaning, thus making the verb mean,

"I have crucified myself together with Christ." The first person passive indicative would be *sunestaurṓthēin*, I have been crucified. In the previous verse is the verb *apéthanon*, I died, the aorist active indicative of *apothnḗskō* (599), to die. It indicates a voluntary, active dying. Thus verse 20 should read, "I have crucified myself together with Christ: nevertheless I live; yet not I [*oukéti* with the absolute *ou*, not], but Christ lives in me: and the life which I now live in the flesh, I live by the faith of the Son of God, who loved me, and gave Himself for me." This is a voluntary crucifixion with Christ which can be corroborated by Galatians 5:24 which says, "And they that are Christ's crucified [*estaúrōsan*, the aorist active indicative of *stauróō*, to crucify] the flesh with the affections and lusts." That is what Paul means by the expression " . . . but the body for the Lord, and the Lord for the body." As our bodies were crucified with Christ on the cross, so we must crucify our old selves with Him (Rom. 6:6; Gal. 2:20).

It is imperative, therefore, that we present our bodies a living sacrifice, holy acceptable unto God (Rom. 12:1).

LESSONS:

1. God made it so that "the belly" is the primary organ in the body where food is digested. We cannot change the process if we want to live a good, healthy life.
2. It will not always be so, as it was with the resurrection body of the Lord Jesus. He ate to live during His incarnation but not after His resurrection.
3. While eating is a necessity, sexual activity is not, and we are explicitly commanded to abstain from fornication (1 Cor. 6:18).
4. The body of the believer is for the Lord and the Lord for the body of the believer. He who gave His life for its redemption is able to keep the believer from sinning, of which fornication is explicitly forbidden (Eph. 5:3; Col. 3:5; 1 Thess. 4:3).

1 Cor. 6:14 — The Lord's Resurrection and Ours

And God both raised up the Lord, and us will He raise up out of the dead through His power.

Why does Paul associate the resurrection of Jesus Christ and our own resurrection with the discussion regarding the necessity to keep the body pure? At first, it seems to be entirely unrelated, but the opposite proves true when we examine that both our resurrection and that of Jesus Christ have to do with the body.

Our Resurrection Body Will Be Governed by Our Spirit

The body is called a natural body (*psuchikón* [5591], natural; *sṓma* [4983], body) having a living soul, contrasted to simply a material substance. After death, the believer is raised a spiritual body (1 Cor. 15:44).

The first thing that we must understand is that here on earth the body is under the control of the soul which we as believers share with animals and unbelievers. It is God's will, however, that the soul of a person be under the control of the spirit, which only man possesses. When a man is redeemed by God's grace, the spirit should take control of the body/soul element.

The second thing to understand is that this change in the status of the animated body now on earth and then in heaven will be constitutional. The body in its changed form in heaven will not be able to be given to fornication. The redemption of our bodies will be then completed. As Paul says in Romans 8:23, we are looking eagerly forward to the "redemption of our body." The word here translated "redemption" is *apolútrōsis* (629). It comes from *apó* (575) meaning "from" or denoting completeness, and *lútrōsis* (3085), redemption. The four occurrences of the word *apolútrōsis*, complete redemption, connect it with the Second Coming of the Lord Jesus (Luke 21:28); the final complete redemption of our present bodies (Rom. 8:23); the day of our complete redemption (Eph. 4:30); and the day of the resurrection (Heb. 11:35). The spiritual redemption enjoyed by the believer now during his earthly life will be made complete (*apolútrōsis*) when his corruptible body will be made incorruptible (Rom. 8:23; 1 Cor. 15:52–55).

Our bodies now must be willfully subjected to holiness or sanctification (*hagiasmós* [38]), part of which is the abstaining from fornication (*porneía* [4202]; 1 Thess. 4:3, 4). When we receive our resurrection bodies, they will be absolutely redeemed and will be constitutionally subject to the spirit instead of the soul.

The Conformity of Our Earthly Bodies to Holiness Will Prepare Them for the Comforts of Heaven

Since our resurrection bodies will somehow be identified with our present earthly bodies, we are advised to keep our bodies unto the Lord and the Lord unto our bodies and have no part in fornication at all. Could it be that our future bodies will be marred by the willful sin that we may bring upon our present earthly bodies? This may be part of the "good or bad" for which we shall be judged. This is found in 2 Corinthians 5:10: "For we [the believers] must all appear before the judgment seat of Christ; that every one [*hékastos* {1538}, each one individually] may receive the things done in his body [this earthly body], according to that he has done, whether it be good or bad." To have given the body to fornication is one of the sins of the body. If we are convicted about such sin and truly repent and confess it, we are assured that there will be forgiveness (1 John 1:9; 2:1, 2). If we do not confess it, we shall be held accountable for it. If we are *pórnoi* (4205), fornicators or practice fornication as a life style, we cannot have the seed of God in our hearts nor are we born again (1 Cor. 6:9; 1 John 3:9).

As Christians, our present bodies should be dedicated to the Lord (Rom. 12:1, 2), for it is the same God who raised the Lord who will also raise our bodies. "But [the] God [referring to the Father] both raised up the Lord, and will also raise us up from among the dead by His own power." The consideration of the future ought to regulate our present behavior in the body. Will our bodies have upon them the marks of any unconfessed fornication?

All Three Persons of the Triune God Had a Part in the Resurrection of the Lord

Let us consider first God the Father. In Acts 4:10 we read, "Be it known unto you all, and to all the people of Israel, that by the name of Jesus Christ of Nazareth, whom you crucified, whom God [**the** God, that is, the Father {cf. John 1:1b}] raised from the dead, even by Him does this man stand here before you whole" (Gal. 1:1; Eph. 1:17, 20; 1 Thess. 1:10).

Then we find that the Lord Jesus Christ raised Himself from the dead: "No man taketh it [My life] from Me, but I lay it down of Myself. I have power to lay it down, and I have power to take it again" (Matt. 26:61; 27:63; John 10:18; see also John 2:19). "But now is Christ risen [*egḗgertai,* the passive form with middle meaning of the verb *egeírō* {1453}, to raise, that is, He has raised Himself] from the dead, and become the first fruits of them that slept" (1 Cor. 15:20; see also Rom. 8:34).

Also, the Holy Spirit raised Jesus. "But if the Spirit of Him that raised up Jesus from the dead dwell in you, He that raised up Christ from the dead shall also quicken your mortal bodies by His Spirit that dwells in you" (Rom. 8:11).

The Body of Jesus

The body of Jesus was without sin. It was *hósion* (3741), sacred, and as such it never saw corruption (*diaphthorán* [1312]; Acts 2:27, 31). The body of Jesus, although it knew no sin, bore our sin, for He was made sin for us (2 Cor. 5:21). His death was real (1 Cor. 15:3, 4) involving His body which was sacred, and it was worthy of the resurrection.

It was His body that was changed to a different constitutional form. "After that He appeared in another [*hetéra* {2087}, other but different as contrasted to *állē* {243}, other of the same kind] form [*morphḗ* {3444}, nature and not just *schḗma* {4976}, shape] as they walked, and went into the country" (Mark 16:12). And yet later in verse 14, we find that "He appeared unto the eleven as they sat eating, and upbraided them for their unbelief and hardness of heart, because they believed not them which had seen Him after He was risen."

Our text says, "And [the] God [the Father] both [*kaí* {2532}, both, even, and] the Lord did raise . . . out of the dead through [*diá* {1223}] His power." The Greek word for "power" is *dunámeōs* (1411) which indicates effective power or exercised power, that is, power that accomplishes its end as contrasted to *ischús* (2479), inherent power not necessarily demonstrated in its achievement.

There was exercised power in the resurrection of our Lord. Observe that in spite of the fact that the change pertained to the body of Jesus, He is called Lord (*Kúrios* [2962], supreme in authority, controller, master). From Jesus Christ, the Man-God, He became Christ Jesus, the God-Man, and He was called this only after His resurrection. We first find this nomenclature in Acts 19:4 and then after that in the Epistles (Rom. 3:24; 8:2, 39; 15:5; 1 Cor. 1:2, 30; Gal. 3:26; 4:14; Phil. 2:5; 3:3, 8; Col. 1:4; Heb. 3:1).

The Resurrection Body of Jesus Was Identifiable

That Jesus was Lord is clearly and explicitly spoken of in Romans 4:24: "But for us also, to whom it shall be imputed, if we believe on Him that raised up Jesus our Lord [*Iēsoún tón Kúrion hēmṓn*] from the dead." This declared that Jesus, born of the Virgin Mary (Matt. 1:25), conceived of the Holy Spirit (Luke 1:26–35), and born after nine months of normal gestation (Luke 1:39–45; 2:6); the One who spoke as no other and did miracles as no human did which included the resurrection of three people (Matt. 9:23–25; Luke 7:11–17; John 11:43, 44), was raised from the dead. At a definite time, three days after He died, deity gave Him a resurrection body that was different than His preresurrection one. It could not be restricted by matter. He was Lord before His resurrection (Col. 2:9), but He took on His resurrection body on the third day. However, He did not become a spirit without a body as prior to His incarnation, but a spirit with a different body, not restricted by matter. How else could He prove that He was the same person to us who can only recognize personality in human form?

He Will Raise Not Only Our Bodies, but Our Personalities

That same power (*dúnamis*) will raise us. Although we were not sinless as He was (Heb. 4:15; 1 Pet. 2:21, 22), yet He was made sin for us: "For He [God the Father] made Him [Jesus Christ] to be sin for us, who knew no sin; that we might be made the righteousness of God in Him" (2 Cor. 5:21). The "us" (*hēmás*) refers to the believers washed in the blood of Jesus Christ. It is noteworthy that Paul does not say "our bodies," but "us." He will make of us something that we were not before. Part of that will be a new body with qualities that our present bodies do not possess. It will be delivered from corruptibility.

First Corinthians 15:42–44 tells us how our resurrection will be affected: "It [the body] is sown in corruption [*phthorá* {5356}, corruptibility]; it is raised in incorruption [*aphtharsía* {861}]."

Fornication Deprives the Body of Its Attributed Honor

The word for "corruption" is *atimía* (819) which means dishonor, not giving the proper honor (*timḗ* [5092], value) or attributed value as contrasted with *axía*, real value, from which the adjective *áxios* (514), worthy, is derived. This is the little value our soul has attributed to our body as if it were not worth our keeping it holy. The body of Jesus was *hósios*, holy, sacred. Our souls should be directed by our God-given spirit, and not by the animalistic *psuchḗ* (5590) or soul which is common to all humanity, believers and unbelievers alike (Rom. 8:4–11).

"It is raised in incorruption" or glory (*dóxē*, the dative of *dóxa* [1391], glory, dignity, the right recognition, which comes from *dokéō* [1380], to think or recognize the right value). The body is said to be spiritually considered lightly during our earthly life, not adequately appreciated by our soul which is affected by sin. Therefore, it may be given to fornication not realizing that it is precious and ought to be given to sanctification (*hagiasmṓ*, the dative of *hagiasmós*, attributed holiness as contrasted to *hagiótēs* [41], inherent holiness only found in Heb. 12:10 and attributed to the Lord alone]) and honor (the dative of *timḗ*, attributed value).

Our souls have not always directed our bodies properly to follow the prescribed explicit and implicit rules of function. There are explicit rules that pertain to sexual relations which are not a matter of choice, but of obedience to specific, divine commands spelled out by God. It is His will that a male and female live together "as one flesh" (Matt. 19:4–6; Mark 10:7, 8; 1 Cor. 6:16) in the bond of marriage. Fornication, that is, relations outside of this prescribed limited circle, is forbidden by the One who made the body. If a person chooses to disobey God's will, he will have to bear the consequences. Man needs to be born again in order for the Spirit of God to control his spirit so that it will act as a restraint against the desires of the body. When we understand the true value of our bodies, we shall keep them in sanctification and honor. The dishonor (*atimía*) with which the body is sown includes the dishonor brought about by both Adam's sin and our own. Thus when it goes into the ground in death, which is its separation from the spirit, it is corruptible. For those who have lived a life of unbelief, there is total and complete dishonor.

Resurrection for the unbeliever is going to be a resurrection of judgment (John 5:29b), but for the believer, it is going to be a resurrection of life (John 5:29a). For both believers and unbelievers, however, there is going to be a judgment as to the degree of personal dishonor brought upon their bodies. For the believer, there will be an accounting as to how he cared for his body while on earth (2 Cor. 5:10). These are the works of faith. Unbelievers will also be judged according to their works and how they treated the bodies which God gave them (see Matt. 19:23–30; Mark 10:23–31; Luke 8:8; 12:35–48; Rev. 20:11–15).

Believers, however, will receive either rewards or retributions for what they have done in their bodies (2 Cor. 5:10), whether good or bad. In the bad is included the occasional sin in the flesh. If there was confession and repentance, there will be forgiveness (1 John 1:9—2:2). If there is no confession and repentance, there will be retribution (Heb. 10:26). It is in view of this judgment of our life of faith or the judgment of works that "everyone [*hékastos*, each one stressing the individual responsibility] of you should know [*eidénai*, the perfect active infinitive of *eídō* {1492}, to know intuitively, to perceive used with present meaning] how to possess [*ktásthai*, the present middle/passive deponent infinitive of *ktáomai* {2932}, to possess, have under one's control] his vessel [*skeúos* {4632}, here meaning the body) in sanctification and honor" (1 Thess. 4:4). In the previous verse, Paul defines this special sanctification, which is abstaining from fornication.

First Corinthians 15:43 tells us that the body "is sown in weakness [*astheneía*, the dative of *asthéneia* {769}, weakness, sickness], it is raised in power [*dunámei*, the dative of *dúnamis* {1411}]." This word "power" is the same word indicating how our resurrection will be accomplished as stated in 1 Corinthians 6:14: "And us He will raise up by His power [*dunámeōs*, the genitive of *dúnamis*]."

How, When, and Where Will Our Resurrection Take Place?

The resurrection of Jesus Christ is referred to as a historical event (*ḗgeire*, the aorist of *egeírō*, to raise). Our resurrection as believers is yet to come (*exegereí,* the future indicative of *exegeírō* [1825], to raise out of), but it is as certain as history. The apostle Paul presents our resurrection as a certainty because of the resurrection of the Lord Jesus Christ. His is past and proven, ours is future and certain.

"And [the] God both [*kaí*] raised up the Lord." God by His power both raised the Lord and will raise us. It is as if he were saying that His power, which was sufficient to raise Christ, will also be sufficient to raise us (Rom. 1:4; Phil. 3:10). Paul gives the documentation of the Lord's resurrection in 1 Corinthians 15:5. Indeed, the Lord raised Himself and appeared to Simon Cephas (Luke 24:34) and the Twelve and also to other disciples (Luke 24:36, 43; John 20:19–21; 1 Cor. 15:6). His resurrection is a guarantee of our coming resurrection. In 1 Corinthians 6:14 it says, "And God raised the Lord." Here the verb is used in the aorist active, which denotes that He raised Him at a point in time and place that could be proved. It indicates first that He is alive even now; and second that the resurrection occurred in Jerusalem three days after He died and was buried. That same power with which the Lord Jesus was raised will also raise us.

The Lord Will Give to Each One an Individual Body

How can this be? Paul calls a person who asks such a question a fool (*áphrōn* [878]; see 1 Cor. 15:36). He then proceeds to give the analogy of the seed that is sown. If it is an apple seed, it will have the body of an apple tree. Although apple trees have a characteristic identity, one cannot see two apple trees exactly alike. And in 1 Corinthians 15:38 Paul says, "But God gives it a body as it has pleased Him, and to every seed [*hekástō*, the dative of *hékastos*, each one individually] his own [*ídion*, the accusative of *ídios* {2398}, one's own private] body."

Paul then goes on to say that there are various kinds of flesh. There are also celestial or heavenly (*epouránia* [2032]) bodies as contrasted to earthly (*epígeia* [1919]) bodies (see 1 Cor. 15:39–41). Our earthly bodies have similarities, but they also have characteristic differences. So will our heavenly bodies. When we speak of human bodies, we cannot isolate the body from the soul and the spirit. We have all three elements, and in speaking of bodies, we speak of personalities (1 Thess. 5:23). It seems that the Scriptures permit us to deduce that whatever we have submitted our bodies to, that kind of body will be given to us in our resurrection. If we chose primarily the material pleasures of the flesh and did not consider how they would affect others or how they would impact others for God, we shall be given resurrection bodies that will not be totally able to enjoy the presence of Christ in His fullness and the new spiritual environment into which we shall be thrust.

Essentially there are two classes of people in the world, believers and unbelievers. To be a believer, one must have the life of Christ within him. But as there are diverse kinds of believers in the measure of their dedication and maturity, so there will be diverse kinds of believers in heaven. The rewards will be according to our works on earth (Rom. 14:10; 2 Cor. 5:10). As we look forward to our resurrection as believers, we must seriously consider how we allow our present bodies to be used.

When Will This Resurrection of Believers Take Place?

The most definitive answer we have to this question is what Paul wrote to the believers in 1 Thessalonians 4:13–18. He tells us that it will be when the Lord Jesus returns in the sky. Those believers who are asleep (dead) will rise first. Then those who are alive at the time will be transformed. They will be made similar to those who have been raised. This will happen very suddenly and quickly—"in a moment [*atómō* {823}, indivisible time], in the twinkling of an eye, at the last trump: for the trumpet shall sound, and the dead shall be raised incorruptible, and we shall be changed" (1 Cor. 15:52). With the dead believers raised and the living believers changed, all believers will be "caught up [*harpagēsómetha,* the first person plural future passive indicative of *harpázō* {726}, to snatch away or catch up] together with them in the clouds, to meet the Lord in the air: and so shall we be with the Lord." The resurrection of dead believers and the transformation of the living believers will be effected by the power of God (*dúnamis,* accomplishing power).

What is not apparent to the English reader is that the verb which refers to the past resurrection of the Lord is *ḗgeiren,* the past or aorist of *egeírō*, to raise, but when it comes to the future resurrection of the believers, Paul uses the compound verb *exegereí.* This is the future active indicative of *exegeírō*, to raise out of, made up of the preposition *ek* which becomes *ex* because the next word begins with a vowel; and *egeírō*, to raise. This is a resurrection "out of." We have already seen that at the Second Coming of the Lord (*parousía* [3952]), the believers will be taken out of the earth (the risen dead and the living Christians transformed). The preposition which indicates this is *ek*, meaning out of the earth. Therefore, we believe that a distinction should be made between the simple verb *egeírō* referring to Christ and the compound verb *exegeírō,* to raise out of the totality of the people of the earth, referring to the resurrection of believers.

The resurrection is called *égersis* (1454), a raising up. It is found only in Matthew 27:53, and its synonym is *anástasis* (386), a standing up (see discussion of this word in *The Complete Word Study Dictionary: New Testament*).

Anástasis is used of the resurrection of Jesus (Acts 1:22; 2:31; 4:33; 17:18; Rom. 1:4; 6:5; Phil. 3:10; 1 Pet. 1:3; 3:21). It is spoken of the future resurrection of believers (John 11:24; Acts 17:32; 24:15, 21; 26:23; 1 Cor. 15:12, 21, 42; Heb. 6:2).

What will happen to the unbelievers? They will be left behind till the day of their resurrection unto judgment (John 5:29; Rev. 20:13–15).

A Better Resurrection

In Hebrews 11:35 the apostle speaks of a better (*kreíttonos*, better, the genitive of *kreítōn* or *kreíssōn* [2909], the comparative of *kratús*, strong, also of *agathós* [18], benevolently good) resurrection. Chapter 11 in Hebrews is the "hall of faith," the heroes and heroines who defied the death of their bodies believing in the certainty of the resurrection. "Women received their dead raised to life again: and others were tortured, not accepting deliverance; that they might obtain **a better resurrection**." The apostle probably had in mind the widow of Sarepta (1 Kgs. 17:17–24) and the Shunamite (2 Kgs. 4:18–37), the one having her child raised from the dead by Elijah, the other by Elisha.

And in the New Testament we have Jairus' daughter (Matt. 9:18, 19, 23–25; Mark 5:35, 42; Luke 8:40–42, 50–56); the son of the widow of Nain (Luke 7:11–17) and Lazarus (John 11). This resurrection was a restoration to their former lives. They received the revivification of their dead bodies to that life which they had before their deaths. It was not "the resurrection unto life" spoken about in John 5:29a. It was not the resurrection Paul speaks about in 1 Corinthians 6:14. It was not the "better resurrection" obviously awaiting the saints and martyrs of Hebrews 11:35.

What Is the Better Resurrection?

What then is this better resurrection? It is the resurrection when believers are going to have their earthly bodies restored to them; the bodies that have been corruptible, dishonored by us, weak and sickly, subject to our soul instead of to our spirit: There will be a new body which God is going to give us as it pleases Him, a body that is incorruptible, a body that recognizes its value. It will be glorious, splendid, powerful, spiritual (1 Cor. 15:38, 42–49). There is no doubt that in verse 49 the apostle Paul speaks about the body, since he is speaking of the image of the earthly which we shall have put off [*ephorésamen*, the aorist active indicative of *phoréō* [5409], to wear) as if it were an outer garment. We shall put on (*phorésomen*, the future indicative of *phoréō*, to wear as clothing) the image of the heavenly. This implies that the measure of honor we have attributed to our earthly bodies will determine the measure of honor and glory the Lord is going to give to our heavenly bodies. Not all believers are going to enjoy heaven equally, and this is one measure of our future enjoyment of heaven.

Paul describes this concept in 2 Timothy 2:8–13:

> Remember that Jesus Christ of the seed of David was raised from the dead according to my gospel: Wherein I suffer trouble, as an evildoer,

> even unto bonds; but the word of God is not bound. Therefore I endure all things for the elect's sake, that they may also obtain the salvation which is in Christ Jesus with eternal glory. It is a faithful saying: "For if we be dead with Him, we shall also live with Him: If we suffer, we shall also reign with Him: if we deny Him, He also will deny us: If we believe not, yet He abideth faithful: He cannot deny Himself.

As we have the verb *exegereí* used in 1 Corinthians 6:14: "He shall raise us out of" or from among the rest of humanity, in Philippians 3:10, 11 we find the noun *exanástasis* (1815), "resurrection out of": "That I may know Him, and the power [*dúnamis*, effective power, the same as in 1 Cor. 6:14] of His resurrection and the fellowship [*koinōnía* {2842}, partnership, sharing in common] of His sufferings [*pathēmátōn*, the genitive plural of *páthēma* {3804}, suffering, affliction, referring to His voluntary sufferings for our sakes, for He had no reason to suffer for His own sin since He had none], being made conformable unto His death; if by any means I might attain [*katantḗsō,* the aorist active subjunctive of *katantáō* {2658}, to finally arrive at the goal, attain, from *katá* {2596}, an intensive showing finality, and *antáō,* to meet, arrive] unto the **resurrection** of the dead."

Paul says, "if by any means I might attain unto the resurrection of the dead." He expresses this with the Greek *eí pōs* (1513), translated "if by any means" (KJV); "if possible" (RSV); "somehow" (NIV); and "in order that" (NASB). This expression ought to be analyzed. It derives from *eí* (1487), if, the suppositional subjective conjunction of unreality, and *pōs* (4458), somehow, the enclitic particle of indefiniteness of manner. It means that Paul is speaking of the *exanástasis*, the resurrection from out of the dead, the first resurrection (Rev. 20:5, 6; see the entry for *anástasis* [386] in *The Complete Word Study Dictionary: New Testament*). It is the subjective wish that somehow it would include him, although this would not be objectively probable for that would entail his death in the near future. Therefore, Paul is not expressing doubt as to the certainty of the fact of the *exanástsis*, the resurrection from among the dead, but as to the timing of the event as far as he was concerned. Such was the pitfall of the Thessalonian believers which he tried to correct by giving them instruction as to the timing of the event (1 Thess. 4:13–18; 2 Thess. 2:1–12). The word translated "resurrection" in the portion of Scripture quoted above is not the regular and often-used *anástasis*, resurrection. Rather, it is the compound word *exanástasis*, resurrection out of, prefixed with the preposition *ek* or *ex* (1537), out of, the same as the verb *exegereí* in 1 Corinthians 6:14. We have already seen that Paul is speaking of the privileged first resurrection of the believers (1 Cor. 15:23; 1 Thess. 4:16; Rev. 20:5). In Philippians 3:7–9, Paul is speaking of the losses he suffered for Christ. These were voluntary losses he chose to suffer. He could have avoided this suffering, and he would not have lost his salvation. An example was Paul's attitude toward women. "Have we not authority to lead about a sister, a wife, as do the other apostles, and as the brethren of the Lord, and Cephas?" (1 Cor. 9:5). Paul was circumspect. He did not simply do all that he could legitimately do, but the very best that he could, so that he could serve the Lord most worthily.

Paul held the same attitude toward money. Although he was entitled to a salary for his ministry, he decided to forego it and to serve without charge (1 Cor. 9:12–18). No wonder a man like that could say, "Wherefore I beseech you, be you followers of me, even as I also am of Christ" (1 Cor. 4:16; 11:1). Can we say this? It all depends how circumspectly we use that which is in our authority to use; especially in the matter of our desire to have as much as we consider ourselves worthy of receiving from the Lord's treasury, or to use of our own earnings to satisfy our earthly pleasures, or in the use of our sexual desires.

One may wonder that if the Lord calls believers to a resurrection out of the human race (*exanástasis* and *exegereí*), He may also have a second *ek* or *ex* from among the ranks of the believers. Remember in the parable of the laborers in Matthew 20:1–16 when it came to dispensing the rewards, the ones who were called first were the ones who were considered as having rendered the least service. Those who only worked for a promised reward were disappointed and thought they should have received more.

We should not forget that Paul was expecting his reward from "the righteous judge" (2 Tim. 4:8). It is part of God's justice to reward those who sacrifice themselves and their comforts and live a holy life for His sake.

LESSONS:

1. The Father raised the Lord Jesus Christ. It is a fact of the past well attested (1 Cor. 15:4–8).
2. This makes the prophecy of our resurrection believable, and this is why it is in the indicative future.
3. God will raise the believers out of all humanity (1 Thess. 4:13–18), as the compound verb *exegereí*, "raise out of" with the prefix *ek* or *ex*, out of, indicates.
4. The resurrection of believers will give them new bodies that will bear the marks of their earthly lives.
5. The believers who in this life simply obeyed and trusted Christ in meeting specific needs in the world, without the promise of specific compensation, will be called first and will be astonished at the generosity of the Rewarder.

1 Cor. 6:15 | Our Bodies Belong To Christ; Keep Them Holy

Do you not perceive that your bodies are the members of Christ? Shall I then, if I were to remove the members of Christ, make them the members of a harlot? Let it never be!

"Do you not perceive? . . ." In Greek *ouk* ("not") is the absolute negative *ou* (3756) which is followed by the consonant *k* because the next word starts with a vowel. *Oídate* is the perfect of *eídō* (1492), to intuitively know, perceive, used as a present tense. The knowledge that our bodies are members of Christ is not something that a believer must learn by experience (*ginṓskō* [1097]), but something that he comes to realize as a result of his relationship with Jesus Christ.

What happens when one truly believes on the Lord Jesus Christ and receives Him? He becomes a child of God, for the life of God is born in him and he is thus born again (John 3:1–12). He receives a life that he did not have before in addition to his natural life. This is called eternal life. "Whosoever is born of God does not commit sin; for His seed remains in him: and he cannot practice sin, because he is born of God" (1 John 3:9).

Christ in Us and We in Him

This mystical transaction is not only Christ in us, but we in God (John 15:4; 1 John 4:13–16). Paul asks the question, "Do you not know [*epiginṓskete*, the second person present active indicative of *epiginṓskō* {1921}, to experientially know with confirmation, to know assuredly as a result of your own experience] your own selves, how that Jesus Christ is in you? . . ." (2 Cor. 13:5, cf. Gal. 4:19). Paul in Colossians 1:27, 28 calls this phenomenon a mystery—"Christ in us."

It is also "we in Christ," for all the believers are members of the body of Christ. We are in Christ Jesus (Rom. 8:1). "But of Him [God the Father] are you in Christ Jesus" (1 Cor. 1:30, cf. 1 John 3:24; 5:20). Paul in his elaboration of this mystery of the body of Christ calls us its members: "Now you are the body of Christ, and members in particular" (1 Cor. 12:27). When we are saved, the Holy Spirit baptizes us into the body of Christ (1 Cor. 12:13). This relates us immediately to each other (1 John 5:1). In Ephesians 1:22, 23 Paul speaks of the church as His body for the church is believers: "For the perfecting of the saints, for the work of the ministry, for the edifying of the body of Christ" (Eph. 4:12, cf. Col. 1:18, 24).

Desecrating the Body of Christ

Since we are spirit, soul, and body (1 Thess. 5:23), how dare we separate the body from our soul and spirit and make it a part of a harlot! We cannot claim that the body acts on its own, for it is a unit, part of our personality. The body without the soul is a corpse, and corpses do not commit fornication. When we allow our bodies to be united to a harlot, we must realize what we are doing. Not only do we make our own body a member of the body of a harlot, but we make a member of Christ a member of a harlot. Therefore, fornication is a gross sin, a desecration of that which Jesus shed His blood to cleanse. Paul intimates that fornication is not like food, which is a natural requirement. Nevertheless, even the consumption of food should be circumspectly regulated. But fornication involves making the body which we claim as our own, but in reality belongs to Christ, a member of a harlot.

In the Old Testament the temple is the designated dwelling place of God. As such, no unclean nor impure thing was allowed to enter it, for His temple was not to be defiled. In 1 Corinthians 6:19 Paul states that our body is the temple of the Holy Spirit. As such, it is to follow God's instructions for its restricted function within marriage. Therefore *porneía* (4202) is the exercise of the sex instinct outside of marriage. To have relations with one's spouse is not fornication (1 Cor. 7:5). In Acts 15:20, 29 we are told to abstain (*apéchesthai*, the present middle infinitive of *apéchō* [568], to be far from, abstain) from fornication, and in 1 Corinthians 6:18 we are commanded to "flee fornication."

Pórnē (4204) is a professional harlot (Luke 15:30; Heb. 11:31; James 2:25). In the city of Corinth the harlots had their heads shaven so that they could be easily recognized for moneymaking purposes (1 Cor. 11:1–16). Consequently, it was easy to flee from them.

Is it possible to be saved from the practice of fornication? Of course it is. Christ said, ". . . Verily I say unto you, That the publicans and the harlots [*pórnai*] go into the kingdom of God before you . . . but the publicans and the harlots believed Him" (Matt. 21:31, 32). In Hebrews 11:31 a harlot is named among the heroines of the faith: "By faith the harlot Rahab perished not with them that believed not, when she had received the spies with peace" (cf. James 2:25).

The Act of Fornication

Is a single sin of fornication sufficient to cause a believer to perish? Not if there is recognition of the sin and abandonment of it. There is no sin that cannot be confessed and forgiven (1 John 1:7–10; 2:2). The blood of Jesus Christ cleanses from **all** sin. However, a truly born-again believer cannot be a member of the body of Christ and practice the sin of fornication. First Corinthians 6:9 clearly states that whoremongers (*pórnoi* [masculine]) will not inherit the kingdom of God. But in verse 11 Paul says, "but such were some of you." The use of the past tense indicates that it was no longer practiced.

The nonbeliever frequently commits fornication with the claim that it is his own body, so he can do what he wants to do with it. The human law goes so far as to absolve him of involving another person as long as that other person is a consenting adult. It is considered evil and wicked according to the law only if it is rape, if that other person is incapable of deciding for oneself or if he or she objects. The consciousness of sin is a concept which imbues the child of God. Thus the believer asks, "Shall I then take the members of Christ, and make them the members of a harlot? Let it not be!" or "No, never!"

The Supposition That the Believer Can Separate His Body and Make It Part of the Body of a Harlot

The Greek text uses the word *áras*, the aorist participle active of *aírō* (142), meaning to take away, thus making *áras* mean, Can't I detach the permanent members of the body of Christ and make them an independent entity causing them to do whatever I wish? The answer to this question is a categorical, "No, never!" It is an ethical prohibition.

If a believer is not allowed to do it even once, he is definitely not allowed to do it as a practice of life. The believer who has the seed of God in his life cannot practice sin (1 John 3:9), any sin, not even once, as 1 John 2:1 says.

But why is "No never!" expressed by the Greek *mḗ génoito!* The "not" here is *mḗ* (3361), the relative subjective "not" as contrasted to *ou*, the absolute objective "not." The answer is that it is possible that a believer may fall into a particular sin of fornication or adultery, for fornication includes adultery as well as any other violation of human sexuality. It even includes mental adultery (Matt. 5:27, 28). If the fallen believer fully repents and confesses, the blood sacrifice of Christ is sufficient to remove the stain as long as purity is maintained (1 John 1:9; 2: 1, 2).

That You May Not Fall Into the Sin of Fornication Even Once!

The verb *génoito* of "Let it never be" is the third person aorist middle deponent optative of *gínomai* (1096), be. This means let it not happen even once. That is the wish of the apostle Paul even as it is of John who in 1 John 2:1 says, "My little children, I wrote these things to you so that you may not sin." The negative *mḗ* for "never" is used which is relative, and the verb is *hamártēte*, the second person plural aorist subjunctive of *hamartánō* (264), to sin, which has reference to even one single sin, because a believer is liable to fall into sin. A believer does not become sinless, for only Jesus was sinless (Heb. 4:15). "If we say that we have not sinned, we make Him a liar, and His word is not in us" (1 John 1:10).

But the habitual practice of fornication could only be possible if a believer could detach himself from being a member of the body of Jesus Christ. The Lord, however, very explicitly told us in John 10:28, "And I give unto them eternal life, and they shall never perish, neither shall any man pluck them out of My hand." The negatives in this passage are the absolute negatives (*ou*). How is it then possible for the participle *áras* of 1 Corinthians 6:15, "having taken away," to refer to actuality and not a mere supposition? It rather represents a subjective supposition as is the case of the aorist participle *kerdḗsas,* gain, in Luke 9:25: "For what is man advantaged, **if** he gain [*kerdḗsas*, the aorist participle of *kerdaínō* {2270}] the whole world, and lose himself, or be cast away?" In the parallel Scripture of Matthew 16:26, the objective suppositional conjunction *eán* (1437), "if," occurs: "For what is a man profited if [*ean*] he shall gain the whole world, and lose his own soul? Or what shall a man give in exchange for his soul?" The supposition is expressed implicitly with the aorist participle *kerdḗsas*, if he were to gain, or explicitly with the suppositional conjuction *eán*.

In that difficult Scripture of Hebrews 6:1–6, we have the same expression, *parapesóntas* (v. 6), the aorist participle of *parapíptō* (3995), to fall by the wayside, correctly rendered by the KJV as a supposition: "if they shall fall away" (see the note on this passage in the *Hebrew-Greek Key Study Bible*, and the third volume of a three-volume study of James, *The Patience of Hope* pp. 234–255).

"If I took [*áras*, the aorist participle of *aírō*, to take away] the members of Christ's body, shall I make [*poiḗsō*, the future indicative of *poiéō* {4160}, to make] them members of a harlot?" But *poiḗsō* can also be the first person singular aorist subjunctive meaning, "Should I make them?" or "Were I to make them" (Luke 12:17). In such a case the *áras*, having taken, should assume the subjunctive making it a supposition, "If I were to take away." The question then would be a subjective supposition as though it had the suppositional conjunction *eán*, if, meaning, "If I were to take away," or "If I could then take away the members of Christ, should I make them members of a harlot?" This is a reduction to absurdity, or *reductio ad absurdum* as philosophy calls such an irrational thinking process. It is often used by the apostle Paul (1 Cor. 15:14). While the supposition may be absurd, the conclusion is correct. An example of that is, If I were to cause the sun to cease to shine, all men would die. The conclusion that all men would die is correct, but it is based on an erroneous assumption. Now if the supposition is absurd, then the supposed conclusion is also an impossibility based on its impossible presumption, as in the case of 1 Corinthians 6:15. If I were able to take away the members of Christ, supposing I could, should I be able to make them the members of a harlot's body? Because it is such a hideous and revolting thought, the apostle says immediately, *Mḗ génoito*, "Let it never be!"

The expression "Let it never be," or take place, is a Pauline phrase. Studying the passages where he uses these words will help one to understand what things Paul considers totally undesirable and impossible in the Christian life (cf. Rom. 3:4, 6, 31; 6:2, 15; 7:7, 13; 9:14; 11:1, 11; 1 Cor. 6:15; Gal. 2:17; 3:21; 6:14).

Because Man Sinned, Did That Mean That God Proved Unfaithful? Let It Not Be So! Consider David.

The first occurrence is found in Romans 3:4: "God forbid [*mḗ génoito*, let it never be so], yea, let God be true but every man be a liar. . . ." God instituted circumcision as a sign for the Jew (v. 1). This was an indication that the words of God were believed (v. 2), but some of them did not prove faithful (v. 3). Does this unfaithfulness by man prove that such individuals prove God false? Never! *Mḗ génoito*! This does not prove God unfaithful.

Paul then brings a quote of David's prayer of repentance after he committed an act of adultery with Bathsheba. He said, "Against You, You only have I sinned, and done the evil in Your sight: that You might be justified when You speak, and be clear when You judge" (Ps. 51:4). This sin of David brings two things to our attention: that God's word proved true and that God's man, even David the righteous, was not perfect or sinless. It is as if the words of John were repeated: "If we say that we have not sinned, we make Him [God] a liar" (1 John 1:10). As a matter of fact, this is not what we prove; rather, we interrupt our fellowship with Him. We become independent, thinking that we can remove our bodies from Christ and make them the members of a harlot. We prove not our strength of independence, but our unfaithfulness. This is called an act of sin (*hamártēma* [265]), as in 1 Corinthians 6:18. Such was the sin of fornication by David (Rom. 3:4, 25). *Porneía*, fornication, in the life of a believer is an act of sin, not a lifestyle, for no true believer can live a constantly sinful life.

These two places (Rom. 3:25; 1 Cor. 6:18) are the only places in the Epistles that the word *hamártēma* occurs. In Romans 3:4, the quotation of Psalm 51:4 concerns David's fornication; and in 1 Corinthians 6:18 it is qualified as an act of sin. A believer may inadvertently fall into sin, but oh! the horror of it—**if** he does! However, God is not proven a liar in that He promised to keep the believers from falling, and yet they did. "Now unto Him that is able to keep you from falling, and to present you faultless before the presence of His glory with exceeding joy" (Jude 1:24). When a believer falls temporarily into an act of fornication, it does not mean that God proved incapable of keeping him or her, it means that man proved unfaithful. That is why we have so many commandments for watchfulness. "That good thing which was committed unto you," wrote Paul to Timothy (2 Tim. 1:12), "keep by the Holy Ghost which dwells in us" (2 Tim. 1:14).

In the case of David (Ps. 51:4; Rom. 3:4), he was restored. The verse says, "Let God be true." How? "That You might be justified in Your sayings [David confirms that God is proven true, justified, in His words], and might overcome when You are judged." The second part of Romans 3:4, as the first part, is also addressed to God as a confessional prayer of David. This means that God will be judged as to the disposition of the sins of His people. Were His judgments just? How will they be viewed by man in the final analysis? He will overcome in His judgments. He will be proven righteous and be acknowledged as such. These are the rewards and retributions He brought upon His people such as David and others. Have we or have we not confessed our sin as did David in Psalm 51 (1 John 1:1–10; 2:1, 2)?

This, however, is only part of Romans 3:4. In Psalm 51:4 David says " . . . and be clear when You judge." God will judge any act of sin of the believer. His blood sacrifice is sufficient to cover even our particular acts of sin committed in our redeemed state as believers (1 John 2:2; 4:10). He will, however, judge it and forgive it if it is confessed and forsaken (1 John 1:9), and if not, it will be retained for retribution in the day of judgment (2 Cor. 5:10; Heb. 10:26).

LESSONS:

1. Fornication, unlike food, is an explicit sin as declared by God's Word from which we must abstain. Fornication regularly practiced excludes a person from God's kingdom (1 Cor. 6:9, 10, 18).
2. Being saved entails the indwelling of Christ in the believer and the believer in Christ (1 John 3:24). When the Holy Spirit attaches us to the body of Christ (1 Cor. 12:13), He does not do it in a removable manner (John 10:28). Otherwise, we must accept the notion that the Holy Spirit does not know what He is doing, and His work is a work of trial and error.
3. Man cannot undo what the Holy Spirit has done (Heb. 6:4–6). The believer cannot sin habitually, and the man who sins habitually has never been born of God through faith in Jesus Christ (1 John 3:9).

1 Cor. 6:16 | Can the Body Act Independently of Soul and Spirit?

Do you not realize that he who glues himself to the harlot is one body with her? For He says, "The two shall be one body;"

The apostle Paul in verse 15 introduced a supposition with the present participle *áras* (142), to take away: Suppose I were able to take away the members of Christ and make them the members of the harlot. This concerns a hypothetical case of a believer. If a believer joins himself to a harlot, he has supposedly detached his body from the body of Christ and joined it together with a harlot. Let it never happen, Paul says, but suppose the act does take place even once. Suppose a believer yields to temptation and commits an act of fornication or adultery. This was his life before he became a believer, but it ceased to be after he became a true believer. First John 3:9 states that "Whoever is born of God does not habitually commit sin, for the seed of God abides in him. He cannot continually sin, because he has been born of God." But it is possible for a believer to fall into an act of sin. In verse 18, this is called *hamártēma* (265), an act of sin.

Adultery may even be a sin of the mind and not necessarily of the flesh. Our Lord said that whoever continuously looks at a woman to lust after her has already committed adultery in his heart. Does that mean that such a believer who commits a mental act of fornication or adultery loses his salvation and is cut off from the body of Christ?

In the fifth chapter of 1 Corinthians, Paul dealt with a young man, a member of the church in Corinth, who for a time fell into the sin of having immoral relations with his stepmother. Apparently he was rebuked by many and disciplined by the church. It is implied that he repented and asked forgiveness for his sin. The apostle Paul argues in 2 Corinthians 2:3–11 for his restoration to the church of Corinth.

The Believer Must Realize the Seriousness of Fornication

The apostle Paul wants the believer to fully realize what he does in the case of the act of fornication. He takes his body and isolates it from his born-again personality, as if the body were an entirely separate entity. This, however, cannot be done, "For this is the will of God, your sanctification, to abstain from fornication" (1 Thess. 4:3). The holiness which the new birth gives to a believer belongs to the whole nature of man, spirit, soul, and body (1 Thess. 5:23).

Don't you realize what a believer does if he falls into the sin of fornication? asks Paul. We translate the *ouk oídate* as "Don't you realize?" *Ouk* (3756) is the absolute "not" and *oídate* is the second person plural of *oída*, the perfect tense used as the present of *eídō* (1492), to intuitively know, perceive, realize. It is to know as a result of a relationship that is established. This phrase is used for the fifth time in this chapter to express the realization that should come to a believer as a result of his relationship to Jesus Christ. It occurs in verse 2 where Paul asks the question, "Don't you perceive [or realize] that the saints will judge the world?" This is a realization that can come to a believer only. It occurs also in verse 3 where the apostle Paul asks another question, "Don't you realize that we [as believers] shall judge angels?"

Again in verse 9 Paul asks a further question, "Don't you realize [or perceive] that the unjust [among whom the fornicators are included] shall not inherit the kingdom of God?" And then finally in verse 15, to declare the result of such an action, Paul says in essence, Don't you realize that the body of the believer is not something that he can detach from his personality and glue to a harlot, as if they were one body?

The apostle Paul wants the believer to realize that the act of fornication is so abhorrent that he will never allow it, not even in his imagination. By the use of the verb *ho kollṓmenos*, the present passive participle of *kolláō* (2853), to glue, he implies a relationship that is made permanent. This verb, although passive, has middle significance and could be translated, "He that glues himself or attaches himself to the harlot is one body with her." The believer who does this cannot blame it on the weakness of his body and thus reduce his sinfulness. It is an act of the will before it becomes an act of the body.

It is impossible for a believer to adopt the life of a fornicator. The fact that the verb is in the present participle means continuity. It is *ho kollṓmenos*, he who keeps on gluing himself. The sin of fornication becomes a habit. It is desired over and over again and becomes addictive. In 1 Corinthians 6:11 Paul says, "And these things some of you were." The verb is in the past tense. As Christians, you are now finished with the old life whose characteristics are described in verses 9 and 10. Therefore, the statement which he makes in verse 16 must be a statement of fact and continuity. A similar statement is found in verse 17, "But he that is glued [or joined] to the Lord is one spirit." Here we have the attachment to the harlot and the attachment to the Holy Spirit. The harlot attracts and keeps, and the Holy Spirit also attracts and attaches to Christ. The sinner becomes one body with the harlot, and the sinner cleansed and purified by the blood of Christ is joined by the Holy Spirit to the body of Christ and becomes one spirit with Him.

Speaking of Christ, the writer in Hebrews 1:3 says, ". . . after He had made men clean from their sins." This is a cleansing that Jesus Christ does through His Spirit. The one who becomes thus purified cannot be attached to a harlot and thus make his body one with her. Such sin after his cleansing is loathesome to the Lord as it should be to himself.

Marriage Is Not a Life of Fornication

In contrast then, Paul presents what happens in marriage: "For He says, 'The two shall be one body.' " The verb *phēsín,* "He says," is the third person singular present indicative of *phēmí* (5346), to say. Paul does not declare who says it, but it is God or the Scriptures. It is an explicit statement of God that one man and one woman shall marry, and this marriage shall include the union of the one body with his or her spouse: "And they shall be one flesh" (Matt. 19:5; Mark 10:8; Eph. 5:31). Marriage is an attachment according to God's law, and therefore the sexual relations between husband and wife are not sinful but a duty as Paul states in 1 Corinthians 7:3–5.

Marriage Is Sacred: One Man to One Woman and No Others

The apostle Paul stresses the difference between fornication and the union of one man and one woman who become husband and wife. There is the union of two bodies into one flesh which is legitimate and does not constitute fornication. Any deviation from that norm demonstrates human nature apart from God. It is true that marriage includes the attachment together of the bodies of husband and wife, but it is not the bodies only that are joined together, but their whole personalities. In Matthew 19:5 Christ said, "For this reason shall a **man** forsake his father and mother, and shall cleave [*proskollēthēsetai*, shall glue himself to, the third person singular future middle/passive indicative of *proskolláō* {4347} from *prós* {4314}, to, and *kolláō*, to glue] to **his wife**: and the two shall be one flesh." It is man who attaches himself to his wife, and that is ordained of God and is not fornication. The Greek word for "harlot" (*pórnē*) comes from the verb *pernáō*, to sell. Harlots were selling their bodies as merchandise. In the New Testament "to sell" appears as *pipráskō* (4097), to dispose of as merchandise. Therefore, a harlot is a prostitute who sells her body to make money (Sept.: Gen. 38:15; Josh. 2:1; Matt. 21:31, 32; Luke 15:30; 1 Cor. 6:15, 16; Heb. 11:31; James 2:25). There is a difference between a harlot (*pórnē*) and a wife (*gunḗ* [1135]; see Sept.: Gen. 24:3ff.; Matt. 5:31, 32; 14:3; 18:25; Mark 6:18; Luke 1:18, 24; 8:3; Rom. 7:2; 1 Cor. 7:2). The union of a man with a woman as his wife is a wonderful earthly mystery (Eph. 5:31, 32). It is the union not of two bodies alone, as is the case with a prostitute, but of two human beings, a male and a female, and this includes their spirits and souls in addition to their bodies. The apostle Paul calls this a mystery demonstrating the greater mystery concerning the union of Christ and the church.

LESSONS:

1. Marriage is God-ordained.
2. It is two lives glued together into one.
3. A sexual relation outside of marriage is fornication.
4. Fornication, as a lifestyle, is proof that a person is not a believer, for a believer is a member of the body of Christ and cannot indulge in sin.
5. An act of fornication for a believer should be repented of, confessed, and abandoned.

1 Cor. 6:17 | *The Believer's Union With Christ*

But he that glues himself to the Lord is one spirit.

The verb used in this verse is exactly the same verb as is used in verse 16. A contrast is drawn between the person who glues himself to the harlot and the one who glues himself to the Lord.

Marriage Is an Example of Our Attachment as Individuals to Jesus Christ

The differences Paul draws in these verses are indicated by the adversitive particle *dé* (1161), but. It contrasts the manner in which one is attached to the harlot and the manner in which another person is united with the Lord. In both instances, it is *ho kollṓmenos* which is the nominative singular masculine present middle or passive participle of *kolláō* (2853), to glue, to attach or unite. In the first instance, the verb must be taken in the middle voice which means "he who glues himself." The same form, however, can refer to the passive voice. The believer is glued to the Lord. This is accomplished by someone other than himself. Here in verse 17, it is the Spirit of God who glues the believer to the Lord (1 John 4:13). A man may be attracted to Jesus Christ by mere persuasion as to His supremacy and power, which is demonic faith (James 2:19). True faith is prompted and effected by the Holy Spirit (John 3:16). It is the second kind of faith that is exercised by the person referred to in verse 17. This is an initial attachment to Jesus Christ that involves the power of the Holy Spirit making the man a sheep of the Great Shepherd. He becomes cognizant and obedient to the voice of Christ and receives eternal life. He is placed in the charge of God the omnipotent Father from whose hands no one can detach him (John 10:27–29). No wonder the apostle Paul considers the earthly marital union as an example of the greater mystery of the union of a human personality with the Lord (Eph. 5:32).

The present participle *ho kollṓmenos* is very much like *ho pisteúōn* (4100), the believing one, in 1 John 5:1, meaning he who continually believes. If the faith is a living, true faith, it results in eternal salvation and life (Heb. 5:9). It is not a struggle of the true believer holding on to the Lord. Once he puts his faith in the Lord, it is the Lord who takes over in the initiation, the preservation, and the perfection of that faith.

Oneness in Christ

Something mysteriously excellent takes place during regeneration which the apostle Paul describes in Romans 8:8–11:

> So then they that are in the flesh cannot please God. But ye are not in the flesh, but in the Spirit, if so be that the Spirit of God dwell in you. Now if any man has not the Spirit of Christ, he is none of His. And if Christ is in you, the body is dead because of sin; but the Spirit is life because of righteousness. But if the Spirit of Him that raised up Jesus from the dead dwells in you, He that raised up Christ from the dead shall also quicken your mortal bodies by His Spirit that dwells in you.

The oneness that exists between the believer and Christ is like the oneness that exists between God the Father and God the Son, the Lord Jesus Christ, for He Himself in John 17:22 said, "And the glory which You gave Me I have given them, that they may be one, even as We are One."

"To the Lord" (*tṓ kuríō,* the dative of *ho kúrios* [2962], the Lord, the Supreme Sovereign of the universe) refers to the Lord Jesus Christ (Mark 16:19, 20; Acts 19:10; Eph. 5:10; Col. 3:23; 2 Thess. 3:1, 5; 2 Tim. 4:8; James 5:7). Paul in 2 Corinthians 3:17 says, "Now the Lord is that Spirit: and where the Spirit of the Lord is, there is liberty." Therefore, he that is united to God is free, and his freedom is bound by the Holy Spirit so that it is not an effort for him to be attached to the Lord Jesus, but it is the natural result of the work of Christ in his heart. As John says in 1 John 3:24, "He that keeps [*ho tērṓn*, the present participle of *tēréō* {5083}, to keep] His commandments abides in Him." The one who abides in Christ finds it easy, in fact, a pleasure, to keep His commandments for His commandments are not burdensome (*bareíai*, the nominative plural feminine adjective of *barús* [926], heavy; see 1 John 5:3).

When we constantly attach ourselves to the Lord we become one spirit with Him. We cannot have our own spirit reigning within us and also His Spirit, but since His Spirit is all knowing, all powerful, and all discerning, we are better off with His Spirit being preeminent within us. This is the baptism of the Holy Spirit which begins with our new birth, "For by one spirit are we all baptized into one body, whether we be Jews or Gentiles, whether we be bond or free; and have been all made to drink into one spirit" (1 Cor. 12:13). Twice the Holy Spirit is referred to as a seal (Eph. 1:13; 4:30). As we live with the Holy Spirit in our hearts, we have the guarantee that we have been accepted as members of the body of Christ. This seal of ownership is found also in 2 Corinthians 1:22. The Holy Spirit is God's guarantee that we will be taken into our Father's house to be His forever.

<u>LESSONS</u>;

1. The believer's relationship with Christ is a spiritual oneness.

2. The closest parallel relationship is that of the union of a husband and a wife.
3. The marriage relationship is a soul and body relationship.
4. The relationship with Christ is not a burden, but rather a joy.

1 Cor. 6:18 — *Fornication Is Explicitly Forbidden*

Flee fornication. Every act of sin, which if a man were to commit, is outside the body, but he who commits fornication sins unto his own body.

Christianity cannot totally isolate itself from the rest of society, and so the danger of moral delusion is always present. It was the prevalence of immorality that made Paul write to the Corinthians, "Flee the fornication." The very fact that the pagan gods were represented as prone to sensuality had a degrading influence on any kind of morality. There was a common saying that, "If the gods do it, [commit fornication], why should not we as men?" Especially in Corinth was prostitution so widespread that it made the apostle Paul give constant warning to the Christian to flee from it. The teaching of the apostle is that the practice of fornication excludes a person from the kingdom of God (1 Cor. 6:9). Even the temporary sin of fornication is cause for exclusion from a local church (1 Cor. 5:2).

The verb that is used and translated as "flee" is *pheúgete*, the second person plural present active imperative of *pheúgō* (5343) which means to flee in order to escape, to run or move hastily from danger because of fear. The present imperative indicates that we must constantly run away from it.

Fornication Elicits an Explicit Prohibition

The noun *porneía* (4202), fornication, has the definite article *tḗn* (the feminine accusative of *ho* [3588]) in front of it. Paul says, "Flee **the** fornication" which indicates that it was **the** vice and **the** practice with which the Corinthians were well acquainted. In 1 Thessalonians 4:3 where Paul says, "Abstain [*apéchesthai*, the present middle infinitive of *apéchō* {568}] from **the** fornication," the definite article is also used.

It seems that the place where the sacrifices for idol worship were made was the place where one was enticed to fornication. That is why Paul in 1 Corinthians 10:14 says, "Wherefore my dearly beloved, flee from idolatry." It is a sad state of affairs when the true God who alone is worthy to be worshiped is replaced by a false god as an object of worship. There immorality multiplies. It was true in Corinth and it is true today. In India, for instance, temple prostitutes constitute a caste. This vice and practice of prostitution dates from the earliest times. While the Israelites were in Egypt, they were familiar with the fact that prostitution prevailed in connection with Egyptian cults. No sooner were they settled in Canaan than the purity both of their morality and their religion was endangered by the contaminating influence of Semitic rites in which the consecrated harlot (*qᵉdēshāh* [6948, OT]) played no small part. From Jeremiah 5:7 we understand that adultery and fornication became prevalent among the Israelites and were synonymous with forsaking God and attaching themselves to the gods of idolatry. They even had harlots' houses which proves that fornication was an organized practice. Hosea 4:14 says, "I will not punish your daughters when they commit whoredom, nor your spouses when they commit adultery: for themselves are separated with whores, and they sacrifice with harlots: therefore the people that do not understand shall fall."

One of the blessings of the exile was the extinction among the Jews both of idolatry and religious prostitution. In the Apocrypha, however, we have testimony of the continuance of the common harlot. She haunts the streets (Sir. 9:7) and uses singing as one of her seductive arts (Sir. 9:4). In the time of the Maccabees, the Gentiles in Palestine "dallied with harlots" and had to do "with women within the circuit of the holy places" (2 Mac. 6:4). We have the description of a prostitute's craft described vividly in Proverbs 7:10: "And, behold, there met him a woman with the attire of a harlot, and subtle of heart."

Prostitution in the Days of Christ and the Apostles

The Gospels supply us with little information as to the extent of prostitution in Palestine during the time of Christ. Our Lord rebukes the Pharisees for their hypocrisy in appearing as opposing fornication while they were guilty of it (Matt. 21:31ff.; Luke 7:37–50; John 8:7). In Matthew 21:32 the Lord refers to harlots as a class. The woman of Luke 7, "who was a sinner in the city" (v. 37), probably belonged to the class of harlots. In the parable of the Prodigal Son, the far country in which he devoured his living with harlots (Luke 15:30) might possibly have been within Palestine. Again, our Lord's reference to the sin of fornication (Matt. 19:9) suggests the existence of immoral women.

In Christ's day, society was in many ways demoralized by Greek and Roman influences, for instance, Corinth (1 Cor. 5:1; 6:13, 18; 7:2; 2 Cor. 12:21), Thessalonica (1 Thess. 4:13), Thyatira (Rev. 2:21). Aphrodite was the Greek mythological goddess of love and beauty, identified by the locals with Venus. Smaller cults like that of the Cabiri existed in Chaldea. Sybil existed at Thyatira where tradeguilds were numerous and afforded ample means of corruption.

Almost everywhere the air was tainted, so that to have no part in immoral practices was comparable to leaving the world (1 Cor. 5:10).

Avoid Even What Could Bring You in Association With Prostitution

Fornication was so closely connected to idolatry that the sin and practice of idolatry often included acts of fornication. That is why fornicators are included so often in the groups of idolaters named (1 Cor. 5:9, 10; 6:9; 10:7, 8; Eph. 5:5; Rev. 21:8; 22:15). For this reason, the apostolic decree was issued from the Jerusalem church in Acts 15:29: "that you abstain from meats offered to idols, and from blood, and from things strangled, and from fornication: from which if you keep yourselves, you shall do well."

Each time the Corinthian Christians came to the temple devoted to idols to buy meat, or for that matter also in the open market, it was an assault on their conscience. Paul seems to have been practical minded in allowing the purchase of such meat since generally it was cheaper, but he cautions the Corinthians about the dangers that exist. This is a law of expediency that he expounds, but subjected to the law of the Christian conscience. He recommends that we as Christians consider the weak brother's conscience (Rom. 14:20ff.; 1 Cor. 8:4–13; 10:18). Although the apostle Paul permits the eating of meats sacrificed to idols that are left over and put on the open market, he insists that the Christian should flee from fornication. The Lord in His letter to Thyatira forbids it altogether (Rev. 2:20), because the danger may lead to fornication. The Christians had to break away from the tradeguilds that existed in Thyatira to avoid contamination. The Lord warned them through the example of the Israelites who were tempted by Moabitish women to eat meat sacrificed to idols and to lust at Balaam's instigation (1 Cor. 10; Rev. 2:14).

The Christians of Ephesus are commended for hating the works of the Nicolaitians (Rev. 2:6). These were followers of a man called Nicholas, and are mentioned twice in the New Testament (Rev. 2:6, 15). There was a party at Ephesus and also at Pergamos whose tenets were similar, it seems, to those of Balaam in that they enjoined or permitted laxity in ceremonial eating of food offered to idols and in social morals.

The goddess Aphrodite had a temple dedicated to her at Corinth. Her devotees were called *hieródouloi*, temple slaves. In actuality, they were nothing but prostitutes. They had their heads shaven for easy distinction. They were also called *hetaírai* (the feminine of *hetaíros* [2083], comrade), a name that stood in contrast to a lawful wife. They were comrades or companions for money. Such was the rampant immoral climate of Corinth where it became most appropriate for the apostle Paul to say, "Flee the fornication."

Fornication Begins in the Heart

Christianity opposes fornication in every form, not only in overt acts but even in lustful thoughts. As a preventive we are not only to flee fornication itself, but also the evil thoughts that lead to it. Our Lord, for instance, in Mark 7:21 says, "From within, out of the heart of men, proceed evil thoughts, adulteries, fornications, murders." Paul says that fornication comes from the desire for evil things, from the lusts of the flesh, and from unrighteousness.

There were things that should not even be named among Christians, as also today. Christianity, especially through the teachings of Paul, saw marriage as a preventive measure against fornication. Though desiring the unmarried to remain as they were, yet, rather than run the risk of incontinence or the fire of lust, they were allowed to marry. So strong was the reaction against impurity in a city like Ephesus where John labored that he regards the chaste, unmarried virgins (*parthénoi*, the plural of *parthénos* [3933]) as a select group (Rev. 14:4).

Fornication Defiles the Temple of the Holy Spirit

In 1 Corinthians 6:19 the apostle Paul calls the body the temple of the Holy Spirit, and fornication is called a sin against the body. It is a defilement of God's temple. Fornication, therefore, is a violation of self in a special sense, and God's judgment awaits it. The very idea of sanctification is incompatible with fornication, for it is directly opposite to God's righteousness, and John brands fornicators with the opprobrious terms "dogs" (*kúnes*, the plural of *kúōn* [2965], dog), or defiled (Rev. 22:15).

From the multiplicity of the phraseology of sensual sins in the New Testament, we can gather how widespread and multiform this evil of fornication was, especially in Corinth. Among the many listed, we find uncleanness (*akatharsía* [167]; see Rom. 1:24; 6:19; 2 Cor. 12:21; Gal. 5:19; Eph. 4:19; 5:3; Col. 3:5); licentiousness (*asélgeia* [766], an insatiable desire for pleasure; see Rom. 13:13; 2 Cor. 12:21; Gal. 5:19; Eph. 4:19), often side by side with fornication (*porneía*; see 2 Cor. 12:21; Gal. 5:19; Eph. 5:3). So often is *pleonexía* (4124), covetousness, found along side *porneía* that many are inclined to regard it as itself a form of sensuality, a desire to have more of it. These were regarded as characteristic sins of the heathen.

Paul admonishes his child in the faith, Timothy, to avoid the temptation and the trap of desires which are permitted among the heathen, among which the root of all evil is the desire to enrich oneself (1 Tim. 6:9, 10). After all, the word *pórnē* (4204), female prostitute, and *pórnos* (4205), male prostitute, derive from *pernáō*, to sell. This derives from *peráō*, to pass through, carry over (particularly as merchants), and then to sell, which in the New Testament appears as *pipráskō* (4097). Money is involved, and the desire to receive money by selling one's flesh is the motivating force; therefore, the dictum by the apostle Paul in 1 Timothy 6:10 that the root of all evil is the love of money (*philarguría* [5365]).

Watch What Your Eyes See

The Lord said in Matthew 5:28, "But I say unto you that whoever keeps looking on [*ho blépōn*, the present participle of *blépō* {991}, to behold, look upon] a woman to lust after her has already committed adultery in his heart." The concentration of the eye upon any woman who is not one's wife may lead to fornication. Not only is it a sin to keep looking at what you should avoid, but also to expose more of the body than necessary and thus provide the object of temptation. We should do well to heed the admonition of John in 1 John 2:16 that the lust of the flesh (both watching and exposing), and the lust of the eyes, and the pride of life, are things that lead to fornication. First comes the concentration of the eyes upon a woman other than one's spouse, and then the desire to satisfy the flesh. These are dangerous and sure steps toward yielding to temptation. It is also sinful to dress in a way such as to lead another person into temptation. Then Paul says, "Every act of sin [*hamártēma* {265}, an act of sin, not *hamartía* {266}, sin in general; the suffix *–ma* indicates the result of a certain action, in this case *hamartía*] which if [*hó*, the accusative singular neuter relative pronoun of *hós* {3739} which; *eán* {1437}, if, the suppositional conjunction of reality indicating that there is a real possibility] he would do [*poiḗsē,* the third person singular aorist active subjunctive of *poiéō* {4160}, to commit, do] is outside the body, but he who commits fornication [*ho porneúōn*, the present active participle of *porneúō* {4203} indicating the act of fornication at any time] sins unto his own body." The apostle Paul wants to impress that both the one who commits fornication and the one who receives the act of fornication commit invasive acts as far as their bodies are concerned. Herein lies the difference between lusting and committing fornication.

LESSONS:

1. Corinth abounded in fornication as a way of life.
2. Paul does not command the believers to leave Corinth, but to flee from the prevalent sin of Corinth.
3. Fornication is every sexual sin.
4. It is an invasive sin and involves two persons.
5. The act of fornication is called *hamártēma*, while sin in general is called *hamartía*.
6. Fornication is uncleanness associated with idolatry.
7. Fornication begins with an evil thought born in the heart of a person occasioned by the lust of the eye (Mark 7:22; 1 John 2:16).
8. The fornication mentioned in this chapter deals primarily with going to court over material things because fornication was used also for procuring material gain. One way to avoid fornication is to avoid covetousness (Rom. 1:29; 1 Cor. 5:10, 11; Eph. 5:3; Col. 3:5).

1 Cor. 6:19 | *The Believer's Body Is the Temple of the Holy Spirit*

Rather, do you not perceive that your body is the temple of the Holy Spirit of which you have from God, and that you are not your own?

The translators fail to translate *ḗ* (2228), or, rather, even, which is the particle with which this verse begins. Verse 9 also begins with the same particle where for the third time the question is asked, "Do you not perceive [*ouk,* not, the absolute negative *ou* {3756} which becomes *ouk* because the next word begins with a vowel; *oídate*, the second person plural perfect active indicative of *eídō* {1492}, to know intuitively, used as if it were in the present tense]." The first time the question is, "Do you not perceive that the saints will judge the world?" (v. 2); second, "Do you not perceive that we shall judge the angels?" (v. 3); and then again in verse 9 where before the question "Do you not perceive?" we find the particle *ḗ*. This comes after the realization of two privileges that believers will have concerning the future judgment. First, that they will judge the world and, second, that they will judge angels. This is an understanding that only believers have as to their future privileges. Thus the apostle Paul wishes to persuade believers that they ought not resort to unbelieving judges to solve their differences concerning material things. Therefore, he stresses, "Rather [even] do you not realize that the unjust will not inherit the kingdom God?" This is a more obvious realization than the first two. Thus, we go from the major realization to the minor one.

The Perception of the Sanctity of the Believer's Body

Verses 12–20 of this chapter proceed to deal with the sanctity of the believer's body. In verse 13 we read that the body is not for fornication, but for the Lord. We must clearly remember that the apostle Paul is speaking about the body of the believer and not the unbeliever. And then, in verse 15, he again questions the believer's perception: "Do you not perceive [or realize] that your bodies are members of the body of Christ?" (1 Cor. 12:13). Again in verse 16 he questions, "Do you not perceive [or realize] that he who is attached to the harlot is one body with her?" He elaborates that for the believer this is impossible, because if one's attachment to the body of Christ is real and genuine, no one can detach it and make it the body of a harlot. And then, here in verse 19 he has the final question, "Do you not realize?" The particle *ḗ* makes the question literally, "Rather, do you not perceive?" as if this was the most fundamental and obvious question. "Rather [or even], do you not perceive [or realize] that your body as a believer is the temple of the Holy Spirit?" This constitutes the most fundamental question and realization that a Christian should have as soon as he is born again, that he is indwelt by the Holy Spirit and that he is a member of Christ's body (Rom. 8:8–11; 1 Cor. 12:13).

There are two basic conclusions in 1 Corinthians 6: the conclusion in verse 9 that unbelievers, though they be judges, cannot inherit the kingdom of God, and here in verse 19 that believers are indwelt by the Holy Spirit.

As the believer cannot separate his body from his sanctified personality and make it a part of the body of the harlot, he must also remember that his body is a part of his total personality which consists of spirit, soul, and body (1 Thess. 5:23). Nor can the believer blame his body for his possible sinful conduct. When our body as a believer sins, the whole personality, soul and spirit, also sins. It should be stressed that the apostle here speaks of the body of the believer. He stresses not the possible sin of the body, but the necessary sanctification of the body through the indwelling of the Holy Spirit. The apostle Paul in verses 9 to 11 spoke of the most corrupt sinners whose sins are specified by the acts of the body. The fornicator, the adulterer, the effeminate, and the homosexual all consummate their sin in the flesh. They do so because they are idolaters, they are not true followers of the God whom Jesus revealed and who is Himself the true God (1 John 5:20). They were covetous, greedy, thieves, and drunkards. This pertains to their manner of living and pleasures of the flesh. They were revilers with their mouth and rapatious with their hands. The body is involved in all these sins. Their bodies were defiled and became the expression of the thoughts of their souls and spirits. However, there was a complete washing of that filthy body, soul, and spirit, and there was sanctification and justification for those who believed (v. 11). What God the Holy Spirit did for the entire personality of the believer, He did also for his body. Verse 19 should be read in conjunction with verse 11. The blood of Jesus Christ had to be shed to wash away man's sin to make him holy and acceptable before God. Now the part of the personality that became the expression of his sinful activity, namely the body, has been completely transformed and become so holy that it was considered worthy by God to become the temple of His Holy Spirit. The whole transaction was a spiritual transaction that had its full effect on the body.

The Believer's Body Has Been Created by God and Redeemed by Christ

We cannot but stand in awe before the work of creation and redemption. Nowhere do we find the description of the creation of the body of man so simple and so dignified as in Scripture. In Genesis 1:26 we read, "And God said, 'Let us make man in our image, after our likeness' " And what material elements did God use in forming man? We read in Genesis 2:7: "And the Lord God formed man of the dust of the ground." No material could be more humble or basic. It is not the material used that is important, but the God who used it and could transform it to such an element of dignity. See what God did next: "And breathed into his nostrils the breath of life; and man became a living soul."

But man, as we know, disobeyed God and has suffered the consequence of that disobedience, which is death, ever since (Gen. 3:3–13). The whole personality of man was affected. Man became driven by sin and became natural (*psuchikós* [5591]), motivated by his soul (*psuchḗ* [5590]) which he holds in common with animals. Man thus became driven by his animalistic instincts instead of by the Spirit of God which the Creator originally determined should direct him. As Paul says in 1 Corinthians 2:14, "But the natural [*psuchikós*] man does not receive the things of the Spirit of God: for they are foolishness unto him, neither can he know them, for they are spiritually discerned." Man thought he would become wise and capable of directing his own affairs, but in reality he allowed the devil to control him (John 8:44; 13:2). James 3:15 says, "This wisdom [natural wisdom which man chose instead of the wisdom of God] does not descend from above, but is earthly, sensual [*psuchikḗ*, psychic, governed by the *psuchḗ*, the part of the immaterial life held in common with the animals], devilish [*daimoniṓdēs* {1141}, demon-like]." The almighty God, man's Creator, was thus replaced by another spirit, the spirit of the devil, as his manager. When Paul speaks of the body of man, he does not mean the dead body separated from the soul, but the spiritually dead body being directed by a spirit which is not the Spirit of God, but the spirit of the devil.

The Believer Is Transformed from a Natural Man to a Spiritual Person

In 1 Corinthians 2:14 Paul is speaking of the natural man, and in verse 15 he contrasts him with the spiritual man: "But he that is spiritual judges all things, yet he himself is judged of no man." And then in verse 16 he says, ". . . but we have the mind of Christ." To be saved, to be a believer, is to have the mind of Christ direct the body.

When the body/soul of man is indwelt by the Holy Spirit, it does not mean that he becomes an automaton in relation to the Spirit of God. This is why the commandments for the believer are so explicit that he must flee fornication (1 Cor. 6:18). In Romans 13:12 the apostle is writing to believers when he says, "The night is far spent," meaning that sin is progressing in the world in spite of our presence and activity in it. And then he continues, "The day is at hand [the day of the reward of the believers and of the retribution of the unbelievers, or the day of the Lord]. Let us therefore cast off the works of darkness, and let us put on the armor of light." In Ephesians 4:22 the apostle advises us "that you put off concerning the former conversation [*anastrophḗ* {391}, behavior] the old man, which is corrupt [*ptheirómenon*, the present participle of *phtheírō* {5351}, to waste, to corrupt] according to the deceitful lusts." And in verses 23 and 24 Paul advises positive action: "And be renewed in the spirit of your mind, and that you put on the new [*kainón* {2537}, qualitatively new] man, which after God is created in righteousness and true holiness." When the Spirit of God indwells man as a believer, he becomes a qualitatively new man. He ceases from his sinful lifestyle, but his body/soul does not lose the capacity to commit sinful acts even though this is not the will of God. Thus Paul in Romans 7:20 says, "Now if I do what I would not, it is no more I that do it, but sin that dwells in me," and by the "me" Paul means his body/soul that is redeemed.

The body/soul of man thus becomes a battleground between the Spirit of God that indwells him and the spirit of the world that surrounds him. The victory is assured, but the struggle is real. Along with this struggle is the fact that the saved body of man continues to be subject to the consequences of man's sin in Adam. Although our souls are saved, our bodies still are subject to "the bondage of corruption" (Rom. 8:21) from which our complete liberation is yet to come (Rom. 8:23).

This is the condition of our body which the Spirit of God has deigned to call His temple. In the Old Testament, the temple (*naós* [3485]) referred only to the interior and most sacred part where God was understood to dwell. It was a holy place. As God is conceived of dwelling in a holy place that is material, so He is said to dwell in our bodies which must be kept pure and holy. This is the emphasis that the apostle Paul brings here in the discussion of the believer's behavior as far as his body is concerned. In spite of its imperfections, we must realize that God has made our body to be His dwelling place. But God is a Spirit (John 4:24). The body is material. Nevertheless there is implanted in it life, a new nature, made possible by the sacrifice of Jesus Christ.

Man Is Unique

There is a difference between the body of man and the body of animals or any other living thing. Only of the formation of man did God say, "Let us make man in our image, after our likeness"

(Gen. 1:26); and it was only of men that it was said, "And let them have dominion over the fish of the sea, and over the fowl of the air, and over the cattle, and over all the earth, and over every creeping thing that creepeth upon the earth." The primary difference between the body of man and the body of animals is that the body of man has in it the breath of God. It is related to God and it is expected to follow the rules of life devised by its Manufacturer. In the case of man and animals, there is the common beating of the heart, and the flow of the blood, and the action of the lungs, and so forth. And yet there is a difference, broad and deep and infinite. Scripture presents the difference to our minds and puts upon it a stamp which is a seal of our patent of precedence in the world of life. It tells us that it was God's breath which first filled human lungs, and that human life came by direct communication from God Himself.

This is the dignity of the human body. The deepest and most mysterious ground upon which this dignity rests is the fact that it was assumed and inhabited by God Himself.

Why Did Christ Take Upon Himself a Body?

Think of the dignity of the human body in regard to the incarnation of Jesus Christ, the Son of God. God was always and is essentially spirit (John 4:24). "God was the Word" (John 1:1). There was a time in history when "the Word became flesh" (John 1:14). What was that flesh? It was a human body, although sinless (Heb. 4:15). What an ultimate honor that God should assume a body Himself by becoming man. He was always known as the Son (*huiós* [5207], son in contrast with *téknon* [5043], child). In His Sonship, Christ assumed a body that was sinless. As Paul says in Colossians 2:9, "In Him dwells the fullness of the Godhead bodily." Jesus Christ in his incarnation became truly "the temple of the Godhead." In Him was the divine presence in a manner as in no temple "made with hands" (Acts 7:48; 17:24; Heb. 9:24).

Jesus cared about His body which only in one sense was "made with hands," because a mother was involved as far as His humanity was concerned. He was conceived of the Holy Spirit. In His life He showed fully that He was man and also that He was God. He voluntarily set aside the prerogative of His deity when He wanted to show His humanity, and the prerogative of His humanity when He wanted to show His deity.

He lived, however, giving us the perfect example of humanity when it is indwelt by deity. He took care of the body that He assumed. It became subject to all the weakness and weariness of a poor, hard-working life, and it was crucified and buried, but it also rose again from the dead, and ascended into heaven (Acts 1:9–11). No doubt we need, in addition to physical perception, the eye of faith to appreciate the ascension of the risen body of Christ. It is an event that transcends physical laws. We cannot explain how the human body was put together although we stand amazed at the way it functions. We stand before earthly mysteries that become heavenly glories. Surely there must be laws transcending those physical laws, and we cannot help but believe when we have full evidence of the death, burial, and resurrection of Jesus Christ whose body finally ascended into heaven. This is the ultimate dignity that the incarnation of the Son of God gave to the body. It is our redeemed body that is going to have the same experience of glorification.

The Body of the Believer Receives Divine Dignity

The argument of the apostle Paul here then, is, how can we take this body and commit it to a life of sin? Because there was nothing that we on our own could do to redeem that body, He gave His own body to purchase us from the slavery of sin and corruption (Rom. 8:21). The present, redeemed human body has to struggle through this vile earth until the time that it will be liberated from the corruptibility of its fallen, but redeemed nature, and thus its redemption will be complete (Rom. 8:23; 1 Cor. 15:52–55).

It is incumbent upon us, therefore, to try to conform our earthly bodies to what we shall be in our resurrection bodies. We must press on victorious over sin until we are liberated from the corruptibility of the body. We should realize the sacredness of our bodies as redeemed people, that they are indeed the temple of the Holy Spirit. In view of that glorification, there should be present sanctification.

During His earthly life our Lord was touched by the physical needs of others. Observe the large share of His time and attention that He gave to the bodily needs of man. How easy it would have been to conceive of a teacher so spiritual in his conceptions and his occupations, that the bodily needs of men could never gain access to his heart. Our Lord so believed in the dignity of the human body that He Himself "became in the likeness of man" (Phil. 2:7, 8). We can see in the ministry of Jesus to weak and sick humanity how He must have grieved knowing what could have been had man not sinned and disobeyed God (Luke 13:34). The healing of the sick, the giving of sight to the blind and hearing to the deaf, the restoration of the paralytic, and, in fact, the treatment of every form of human disease, constituted a main feature of our Lord's life. It commended Him as a friend to the suffering, even to those who had no ear for His preaching and did not appreciate His spiritual ministry. Our Lord knew what our bodies were meant to be and what they will be. Meanwhile, however, they continue to reap the consequences of sin.

We as Believers Should Possess as Much of the Holy Spirit as Possible

The next phrase of our verse, "which you have from God," needs careful attention and analysis. After telling us that our redeemed bodies are the temple of the Holy Spirit, the apostle begins to elucidate with the Greek word *hoú*, the genitive singular masculine relative pronoun of *hós* (3739), which. Most of the translators translate *hoú* as if it were *hó*, and thus give justification to render it as a reference to the Holy Spirit. It is either *hó*, which would refer to the Holy Spirit, or *hoú*, which would refer to part of the Holy Spirit. We have the same relative pronoun in the genitive used again of the Holy Spirit in 1 John 3:24: "of the Holy Spirit of which He gave us." The apostle Paul is trying to accommodate the inability of the human mind to understand all that is involved in redemption. Conviction of sin comes through the Holy Spirit. When we believe, the Holy Spirit comes upon us, but the sole body of each believer does not become an exclusive possessor of the Holy Spirit. As a limited human being, we can only conceive of a personality in merely one place at a time. The divine personality, however, differs in that it can be in its fullness in many places at the same time. In Romans 8:9–11 the Spirit is referred to repeatedly, but we find that in verse 9 the definite article is not used in front of the phrases "Spirit of God" and "Spirit of Christ." This means that the Spirit cannot all be contained exclusively in one person or in one place. We, as believers, have of the Spirit of God and of the Spirit of Christ. However, in verse 11 we find that we are indwelt by **the** Spirit which means the totality of the Spirit. This means that when we receive the Spirit, we do not exhaust it, but that we have all of the Spirit that we need for our own lives.

The apostle Paul, therefore, in 1 Corinthians 6:19, wants to impress us with the fact that when we are saved, we have the

Spirit of God indwelling us, which, of course, derives from God Himself. We have all of the Holy Spirit we need, but we have no exclusive possession of the Holy Spirit. We can be indwelt by the Holy Spirit to the extent that we welcome Him into our hearts and lives.

Another noteworthy thing in the statement "of which you have from God" is that the verb *échete,* you have, is the second person plural present active indicative of the verb *échō* (2192), to have, indicating that the needed measure of the Holy Spirit is something that we have at the moment of salvation. And not only that, but we can have "refills," so to speak, all throughout our redeemed lives. It is not something we had in the past nor something we shall have in the future, but something that we constantly have, and it is good to remember that it only comes from God. This is why the apostle Paul says in Ephesians 5:18, "But keep being filled." *Plēroústhe*, be filled, the second person plural present passive imperative of *plēróō* (4137), to fill, indicates that the filling is not once and for all, but that there is an initial filling and then "refills," so to speak. It is the desire of the apostle Paul that we should recognize our need during our whole earthly redeemed life to be constantly filled with and enjoying the fullness of the Spirit of God. Thus we have the baptism of the Holy Spirit, which is when the Holy Spirit indwells us. And thereafter we enjoy the grace of being filled with the Spirit. We might think of it as our water supply which contains a thirst-quenching and life-saving element of life. While we keep drawing as much as we need, the water keeps flowing.

There is only one source of this Holy Spirit which is God. It is to be observed that the definite article is not before the word "God" which indicates deity. It is from God the Father (John 15:26) and is of God the Son, Jesus Christ (John 16:7), and of the Holy Spirit as the third Person of the Trinity (John 16:7).

We Are Not Our Own

"And that you are not your own." The negative here is expressed by the absolute "not" (*ou*) which, because it is followed by a word that begins with a vowel (*éste*, the second person plural present indicative of *eimí* [1510], to be), receives the *k* at the end. This is to stress the absolute ownership of the Lord who indwells us. "Your own" is *heautṓn*, the genitive plural masculine third person reflexive pronoun *heautoú* (1438), his. You are not your own since you are His, redeemed by Him, bought back from the slavery of sin, the purchase price being the blood of the Lord Jesus. This is said so that the believer may realize his absolute slavery to God, but at the same time the greatest possible freedom that he exercises in and through Him. This should be related to the twelfth verse where Paul says, "All things are permissible to me, but not all things are for the common interest. All things are permissible to me, but I shall not be mastered by any." Paul is declaring his complete willful slavery to Jesus Christ and, hence, when he is permitted to choose, he chooses only that which is for the glory of God and the common good, but never for his own selfish interests. He believes that now, as a redeemed man, he is the property of the One who had the ability and the willingness to pay the price for his redemption.

When the apostle Paul says, "You are not your own," he means that, as you are now constituted with your body indwelt by the Spirit of God, your old Adamic nature does not own you anymore.

We Have Been Crucified With Him

The apostle Paul speaks of the crucifixion of the believer together with Christ. The word which shows the act of this crucifixion is *sustauróō* (4957) derived from *sún* (4862), meaning conjointly together, and the verb *stauróō* (4717), to crucify. In Romans

6:6 he says, "Our old man was crucified together with Him, that the body of sin might be destroyed, that henceforth we should not serve sin." The verb *sunestaurṓthē*, the third person singular aorist passive indicative of *sustaurόō*, shows an act of grace by the person of Jesus Christ. That means that on the cross He took our old man, indicating our Adamic nature or our sinful body, and crucified it together with Him. This was inherent in our faith in Him. Crucified means to be rendered dead, and this is what His transforming grace did with our sinful nature. This, however, did not absolve us from all responsibility. In fact, we now have the personal and greater responsibility to individually crucify ourselves with Him. God gives eternal life only to those who believe. Belief starts the crucified life of the believer, and he is born again. This new life that Christ gives involves an individual responsibility which man cannot execute unless he is born again.

We Continue to Crucify Ourselves With Christ

The same word *sustaurόō* is used also in Galatians 2:20. However, there is a difference in the grammatical structure of the verb. While the verb in Romans 6:6 is *sunestaurṓthē* which definitely is the third person passive voice, "it was crucified together with," meaning that the Lord was the One who did the crucifying, the old man was the person that was crucified with Christ, and this took place at a definitive time. That time was the moment of belief in the Lord Jesus Christ. The grammatical structure, however, of the verb *sunestaúrōmai* is the first person perfect passive indicative with middle meaning. Morphologically, the same form of the verb is used for both the middle and passive voice. The passive voice represents the subject as receiving the action of the verb, while the middle voice represents the subject as acting in some way upon himself or on his own behalf. If it is passive the translation would be, "I have been crucified with." If it is middle, then the translation should be, "I have crucified myself." The grammatical structure cannot determine whether it is passive or middle, but only the context and the general theology of the apostle Paul. The context here indicates that this action is taken by the individual in the Holy Spirit. The believer who follows up on the work of Christ is crucifying the old man with the help of the Spirit of God within him. When the Lord thus confronts a person, He also gives him the desire to continue His work of faith, to continue His work of giving eternal life. "I live, yet not I, but Christ lives in me; but the life which I now live in the flesh [*en sarkí*, the dative of *sárx* {4561}, flesh, which is equivalent in this instance to *soâma* {4983}, body, that is, body/soul], I live in the faith of the Son of God who loved me and gave Himself for me." It is apparent here that the subject of crucifixion is the believer who was loved by Jesus Christ and for whom He gave Himself on the cross.

The Responsibility of the Believer

The general Pauline theology concerning the work of Christ and the ensuing responsibility of the believer is demonstrated in Galatians 5:24 when the active voice of *stauróō,* to crucify, is used: "And those who belong to Christ Jesus crucified [*estaúrōsan*, the third person plural aorist active indicative of *stauróō*, to crucify] the flesh with its passions and desires." Here it is evident that Paul is speaking about believers crucifying their fleshly desires or their bodies with Jesus Christ. The believer is doing what Christ did first, for without His crucifying our old man, we could not and would not crucify our flesh with its passions and desires.

When the apostle Paul says, "And you are in no way your own," he refers to the willing renunciation of the flesh, its passions and desires which continue to exist after man believes but which are kept in complete subjugation. When man believes on the Lord Jesus Christ, he passes from a slave of sin to a slave of Christ. This is expressed in 1 Corinthians 6:11 in the phrase "And such things were some of you." This slavery to sin or to Christ is expressed by Paul in the verb *doulóō* (1402), to enslave. Paul says that in our unbelief we were like children "in bondage [*dedoulōménoi*, given to bondage, the perfect passive participle of *doulóō*] under the elements of the world" (Gal. 4:3). However, when we become believers, things change entirely as is expressed by Romans 6:22: "But now being made free from sin and having been enslaved [*doulōthéntes*, the plural aorist passive participle of *doulóō*, to enslave] to God, you have your fruit unto holiness and everlasting life." The free man on earth is the believer who has passed from a slave of sin to a slave of God. His new slavery, however, is a willing slavery of union with God. The believer is one who readily recognizes the presence of the Holy Spirit within him and understands that he does not belong to himself, but to God. Hence, only believers can receive the commandment, "Flee fornication," for only the believer comprehends the loathesomeness of fornication. In 2 Timothy 2:22 Paul, in writing to young Timothy who certainly was a believer, advises him, "Flee also youthful lusts: but follow righteousness, faith, charity, peace, with them that call on the Lord out of a pure heart." So there is a lot of fleeing and a lot of struggling that the believer has to exercise against the evil that flaunts itself in his own heart and in the world. In James 4:7 it is said, "Submit yourselves therefore to God, resist the devil, and he will flee from you."

LESSONS:

1. As believers, we should realize the degrading effect of sin on the body.
2. Having realized the consequences of sin, we must have some understanding of what the body of man must have been prior to sin.
3. We must realize that our body after sin is not what it was before sin.

4. In redeeming it, God has made it fit for a dwelling place for His Spirit.
5. Although our body is sanctified, it is still mortal.
6. To acquire its original status, the body must await the resurrection.
7. The resurrection of our body will bring about its full restoration and hence incorruptibility.
8. The Holy Spirit will fill the believer when he first believes, and then continue to fill him as he makes room for Him. It is the desire of the Holy Spirit to keep infilling and replenishing us.
9. The thrilling realization of a sanctified life is the fact that we do not belong to ourselves, but to the One who purchased us.

1 Cor. 6:20 — *God's Ownership Of the Believer*

You were bought with a price; indeed, by all means then glorify God in your body and in your spirit which are God's.

In the previous verse the apostle told the Corinthian believers that they were not their own. And now he tells them that they are not their own because they were bought with a price.

An Event in the Past

The verb "you were bought" is *ēgorásthēte*, the second person plural aorist passive indicative of *agorázō* (59), to buy. It derives from *agorá* (58), marketplace. The passive voice means that you were bought by someone other than yourself. The aorist indicates an event completed in the past. The verse does not explicitly state who bought the believers, nor does a parallel statement in 1 Corinthians 7:23. This also says, "You were bought with a price," but it does not say by whom. A compound synonym of *agorázō* is *exagorázō* (1805) derived from *ek* (1537), out of or from, and *agorázō*, to buy, to buy out of, to redeem from. In Galatians 3:13 Paul tells us who is the One who bought us: "Christ bought us out from the curse of the Law, being made a curse for us: for it is written, 'Cursed is everyone that hangs on a tree.'" Observe that Paul does not say Jesus bought us out, but

Christ, His divine name, the Messiah, bought us out. If He were a mere human being, He could not have bought us out. Being the divine Christ, the Eternal Word who became flesh, He was able to buy us out by enduring the curse, by hanging on a tree (see also Galatians 4:5). In this verse it also states the purpose of buying us out: "that we might receive the adoption of sons [*huiothesía* {5206}, adoption, sonship]."

The Redemption of Jesus Christ Has a Beginning, But No End

The biblical word for this buying out by Christ is the word "redemption" (*apolútrōsis* [629] which is derived from the preposition *apó* [575], from, and *lutróō* [3084], to redeem). Redemption (*apolútrōsis*) is the work of Christ beginning with the new birth. It is initiated by the Lord Jesus Christ all throughout the various stages of our redemption until the finality of our glorification. That it is Jesus Christ who is fully responsible for the redemption of man from the beginning of his converted life until the end is demonstrated by the apostle Paul in Romans 3:24: "Being justified freely by His grace through the redemption [*apolutrṓseōs,* the genitive of *apolútrōsis*] that is in Christ Jesus." Note that "being justified" is the Greek *dikaioúmenoi*, the present passive participle of *dikaióō* (1344), to justify, which means the constant work of Christ from the beginning to the end in the life of the believer. In 1 Corinthians 6:11 Paul refers to the initial work of Christ with the sinner being washed and sanctified and justified in the name of the Lord Jesus and in the Holy Spirit. The tenses of the verb in that verse are all in the aorist which means that at a certain time in history, the washing away from sin, the sanctification of a life, and the justification were accomplished by Jesus Christ. But this is both an initial and a continuing work of Christ. This on-going work of Christ will one day be completed in the glorification of the believer.

Redemption is like salvation. It has a past, a present, and a future. Titus 3:5 speaks of the historic salvation, the initiation of salvation as "not by works of righteousness which we have done, but according to His mercy He saved us [*ésōsen*, the aorist active indicative of *sṓzō* {4982}, to save, rescue, redeem] by the washing of regeneration and renewing of the Holy Ghost." Second Timothy 1:9 confirms this initial act of redemption or salvation: "Who has saved us [*sṓsantos*, the aorist active participle of *sṓzō*], and called us with a holy calling, not according to our works, but according to His own purpose and grace, which was given us in Christ Jesus before the world began."

Salvation is also an act of God that is continuing in our experience. This we find very clearly taught in 1 Corinthians 1:18 which says, "For the preaching of the cross is to them that perish, foolishness; but unto us which are being saved [*sōzoménois*, the dative plural present passive participle of *sṓzō,* to save], it is the power of God."

A Restoration to a Life Yet Unknown to Us

This salvation which is initially received when we first believe on the Lord Jesus Christ, and continues all throughout our life of belief, is not a complete redemption. The word *apolútrōsis*, redemption, refers predominantly (as also the word *sōtēría* [4991], salvation) to that ultimate salvation or redemption which will spell the end of suffering and death and will initiate the state of the glorification of the believer. The prepositional prefix *apó* (575) should be taken to refer to completeness and to the finality of our being rescued from this fallen world of sin and from our present corruptible body. This, actually, is the meaning of the first occurrence of the word "redemption" (*apolútrōsis*) in Luke 21:28. In this verse, speaking of the time of Jesus' return and the sign indicating His approach, the Lord Himself says, "And when these things begin to come to pass, then look up, and lift up your heads; for your redemption [*apolútrōsis*] draws near." In Romans 8:23 Paul, speaking about the completion of the work of Christ which will culminate in the complete change of our environment and of our present constitution, says, "And not only they, but ourselves also, which have the firstfruits of the Spirit, even we ourselves groan within ourselves, waiting for the adoption, that is, the redemption [*apolútrōsis*] of our body." This is why Paul says in Philippians 1:29, "For unto you it is given in the behalf of Christ not only to believe on Him, but also to suffer for His sake." We, as believers, experience pain, suffering, and even death. We are not exempt from these consequences of sin when we are saved. However, we are victorious in our suffering (Rom. 8:31–39). Paul speaks also of the day of our redemption (Eph. 4:30). In Hebrews 11:35 the apostle calls the day of the resurrection when our bodies will be redeemed (1 Thess. 4:13–18) a better resurrection; meaning better than the resurrections that have been experienced in this life such as the resurrection of Jairus' daughter (Matt. 9:18–26; Mark 5:22–43; Luke 8:41–56), the raising of the son of the widow of Nain (Luke 7:11–17), and the resurrection of Lazarus (John 11:17–44). Such resurrections were merely restoration to this earthly life whereas our full redemption, which is going to take place, would mean to the restoration of a better life than we have ever known. It will be a life full of bliss in an environment that Christ is still preparing for us and which we cannot yet even imagine (Rom. 8:18–23).

When the apostle Paul says in 1 Corinthians 6:20, "You were bought with a price," he refers to the historic act of the cross, the burial, and the resurrection of Christ which meant the purchase of the sinner from sin and its power (John 8:34; Rom. 6:1, 2, 6, 12, 14). However, our complete redemption, which includes the redemption of our bodies, is to be had in the future during the day of our resurrection. Christ died on the cross once, and the complete work of redemption was accomplished by Him (Heb. 7:27; 9:12; 10:10), and He will not be incarnated again to die on the cross a second time (Heb. 6:4–6). Therefore, the purchase is absolutely complete. His redemption was perfect and does not need repeating.

The Price of Our Redemption Was Set by Christ Himself

The completeness of our redemption is implied by the aorist tense *ēgorásthēte*, bought, which is also found in 1 Corinthians 7:23. It is done and finished for all times, and at the consummation of the ages sin shall be put away (Heb. 9:26).

Usually in a business transaction it is the seller who sets the price and not the buyer. In this instance, however, it was the opposite. Jesus Christ is the One who set the price of our redemption. The word "price" in Greek can be expressed by two different words: first, *axía* which does not occur in the New Testament as a noun. It occurs, however, as the adjective *áxios* (514), worthy; the verb *axióō* (515), to deem entitled, and the adverb *axíōs* (516), appropriately, in accordance with its inherent value. The second word is the word used in 1 Corinthians 6:20 which is *timḗ* (5092), value as esteemed necessary by the buyer, attributed value. By this second word Paul declares that Christ paid that which was necessary to redeem man from sin, its power and its presence, and to make that person His very own in which His Spirit could dwell. In order to impress upon us the necessity of abstaining from sin, Peter tells us in 1 Peter 1:18 what that attributed value was: "Perceiving [*eidótes*, the perfect active participle of *oída* {1492}, to know intuitively, to realize; although the verb is in the perfect tense, it is used with present meaning and should be translated perceiving or realizing as a result of one's relation to Jesus Christ] that you were not [*ou* {3756}, the absolute 'not'] redeemed [*elutrṓthēte*, the second person plural aorist passive of *lutróō* {3084}, to redeem] with corruptible things as silver and gold from your vain conduct [*anastrophḗs*, the genitive of *anatrophḗ* {391}, behavior] received by tradition from your fathers." In other words, Peter indicates that silver and gold with which things a man could be bought were not sufficient to redeem him from sin so that he could become a new creature in Christ. Something far more precious was needed.

The Price Was the Blood of Christ

Verse 19 which follows then tells us what the price of our redemption was: ". . . the precious [*timíō*, the dative of *tímios* {5093} which is the adjective of *timḗ*, price] blood of Christ, as of a lamb without blemish and without spot." In Hebrews 2:14, speaking of Christ, the apostle says, "Forasmuch then as the children are partakers of flesh and blood, He also Himself likewise took part of the same. . . ." What is translated "likewise" is the Greek adverb *paraplēsíōs* (3898) which means "in a very close manner but not exactly." This is explained in Hebrews 4:15: He was without sin. Thus, in order for God to redeem man through the shedding of blood, it was necessary to have the Son of God become the Son of man, the Word, and to take upon Himself flesh. However, it was not the flesh of sinful man, but flesh that was similar yet without sin, and thus He shed His blood on the cross of Calvary. Through this perfect sacrifice, He was able to accomplish that for which He became incarnated, that is to buy out (*exagorázō*) or redeem man.

This does not mean simply the changing of the ownership of man, but setting him free by drawing him to Christ. This drawing, however, is not merely deliverance from the hands of an enemy, which in this instance was Satan and man himself, but it is winning him over to Christ and to His kingdom and placing the nature of God within him (2 Pet. 1:4). This is why the Lord Jesus, in speaking to the Pharisees, said, "If, therefore, the Son makes you free, you shall be free indeed" (John 8:36). He who is paid for by the blood of Jesus Christ is not enslaved in any way, but he is the freest creature that could ever live on the earth. His freedom is circumscribed by the indwelling Spirit of God.

In Romans 6:18 the apostle Paul speaks of the slavery to righteousness. The believer, as a result of what Christ did for him on the cross, receives the spirit of doing what is right consistently and always.

Experiencing such a redemption cannot but cause a man to praise God for what He has done for him.

Enablement to Glorify God Because You Have Victory

Next the apostle Paul tells us, "Therefore glorify God in your body." The first thing that we note about the verb "glorify" is that it is the aorist imperative, *doxásate*, from *doxázō* (1392), to glorify. The aorist imperative means that on realizing your liberation in Christ, you ought to begin glorifying God for this great work that He has done. When in the midst of licentious Corinth, Paul tells the Corinthians, When you see all those harlots making themselves visibly identifiable with their shameless and luring conduct, and you are victorious in fleeing fornication, you cannot but turn to God and glorify Him because through His blood you have conquered the power of sin over you. Remember at all times that your victory is due to the redemption Christ purchased for you.

What Does "Glorify" Mean?

The second thing that we ought to examine is the meaning of the word "to glorify" (*doxázō*). It comes from the verb *dokéō* (1380), the future of which is *dóxō* and the aorist *édoxa*. The verb expresses the objective estimate or opinion formed by man concerning a matter. When others see your conduct as a believer, do they attribute that to the indwelling of the Spirit of God in you, and in turn to the work that Christ has done for you? The verb *doxásate*, glorify, means to permit others to see the real reason for your being different in your conduct. Your conduct should never cause others to say how marvelous you are, but how great is God in you. When they see that, they may crave for that work to be done in their own hearts. The imperative "glorify" is followed in the Greek text by the adverb *dḗ* (1211) used as a particle. This gives the sentence an expression of certainty and reality in opposition to mere opinion or conjecture, meaning indeed, then, now. Most of the translators have rendered it as "therefore," but it would have been better if it were translated "indeed."

The word "God" has the definite article in front of it, *tón Theón* (*tón* [3588]; *Theón* [2316]), **the** God, which means God the Father (John 1:1b). This stands in contrast to the idols which did not exist (1 Cor. 8:5, 6). But the sinful men of Corinth did not know God the Father. Unbelievers can observe Him as they observe your life and see the difference that He has made in it.

Our Body Shows What God Has Done in Us

The area that is most observable as demonstrating the change in your life is "your body." The physical behavior is evident, and will motivate them to think about what has made the difference.

The Textus Receptus which is translated by the King James Version and the Majority Text adds "and in your spirit." This, in my opinion, is appropriate because of Paul's statement in the previous verse, that our body is indwelt by the Spirit of God. Therefore, the behavior of the body that others see in the believer is first internal, in the spirit. The body is simply the servant and demonstrator of the spirit.

LESSONS:

1. The purchase of man by Christ was initiated by God.
2. Christ paid the price which would be sufficient not only to free man from his father, the devil, but to attach him to Himself, and thus make him a child of God.
3. This He did historically once and for all, but it becomes a reality experientially in the life of the believer when he believes on the Lord Jesus and receives Him for himself personally (John 1:12).
4. God set the price of man's redemption.
5. That price was the blood of His incarnate Son. Nothing else could satisfy the Father's justice and at the same time change the nature of sinful man (2 Pet. 1:4).
6. The change in redeemed man is observable in the conduct of the body of the believer.
7. This change in the physical conduct is attributed to the converted spirit that begins to indwell man and grows in sanctification.

List of Abbreviations

acc. (accusative)

act. (active)

aor. (aorist [2 aor. for second aorist])

cf. (compare)

ch. (chapter)

comp. (composition)

dat. (dative)

etc. (and so forth)

ff. (following)

gen. (genitive)

i.e. (that is)

imperf. (imperfect)

indic. (indicative)

inf. (infinitive)

KJV (King James Version)

MT (Majority Text)

mid. (middle)

n. d. (no date available)

N. p. (no publisher available)

NASB (New American Standard Bible)

NIV (New International Version)

NKJV (New King James Version)

nom. (nominative)

p. (page), pp. (pages)

part. (participle, participial)

pass. (passive)

perf. (perfect)

pl. (plural)

pres. (present)

pron. (pronoun)

Sept. (Septuagint)

sing. (singular)

TR (Textus Receptus)

UBS (United Bible Society)

usu. (usually)

v. (verse), vv. (verses)

vol. (volume)

Bibliography

General Works

Harris, J. Rendel. *Union With God.* London: Hodder and Stoughton, 1896.

Harvey, Goodwin. "The Body the Temple of the Holy Spirit." In *The Churchman's Pulpit*, Vol. 28. London: Francis-Griffiths, 1913.

Hastings, James. *Great Texts of the Bible: 1 Corinthians.* London: The Waverly Book Company, 1912.

Jones, J. D. *Richmond Hills.* London: Hodder and Stoughton, 1919.

Moberly, R. C., *Christ Our Life.* London: John Murray, 1902.

Morgan, G. Campbell. In *Westminster Pulpit*, Vol. 1. Westwood, New Jersey: Fleming H. Revell, 1956.

Morrison, G. H. *The Afterglow of God.* London: Hodder and Stoughton, 1912.

Moule, H. C. G. *From Sunday to Sunday.* London: Isbister and Company, 1903.

Riggs, Elias. *Notes on Difficult Passages of the New Testament.* Boston: Congregational Sunday School and Publishing Society, 1889.

Robertson, Frederick W. *Fredericks W. Robertson's Sermons*, Vol. 2. London: C. Kegan Paul and Company, 1881.

Spurgeon, Charles H. "Bought With a Price." *The Treasury of the New Testament*, Vol. 3. Grand Rapids: Zondervan, 1930.

Lexicons, Encyclopedias, and References for Greek Readers, from Classical and Koine Greek to Modern Greek

Byzantiou, S. D. *Lexikon tēs Hellēnikēs Glōssēs* (*Lexicon of the Hellenic Language*). Athens: Koromeela, A., 1852.

Demetrakou, D. *Lexikon tēs Hellēnikēs Glōssēs* (*Lexicon of the Greek Language*). Athens: Demetrakou, 1954.

Enkuklopaidikon Glōssologikon Lexikon (*Encyclopedic Glossological Lexicon*). Athens: Morfootikee Hetaireia.

Enkuklopaidikon Lexikon Eleutheroudaki (*Eleutheroudaki, Encyclopedic Lexicon*). Athens: Eleutheroudakis, 1927.

Kalaraki, Michael and Nikolas Galanos. *Iōannou tou Chrusostomou Ta Hapanta* (*Complete Works of John Chrysostom*), 1899.

Liddell, Henry George, and Robert Scott. *Greek–English Lexicon,* as Translated and Enriched by Xenophoon P. Moschos and Michael Konstantinides. Athens: John Sideris.

Megalē Helēnikē Enkuklopaideia (*Great Greek Encyclopedia*). Pursos (Pyrsos), Athens: Hēlios.

Neōteron Enkuklopaidikon Lexikon Hēliou (*New Encyclopedic Lexicon "Hēlios"*). Athens: Hēlios.

Papaoikonomou, George L. *Lexikon Anomalōn Rhēmatōn* (*Lexicon of Irregular Verbs*). Athens: Kagiaphas.

Stamatakou, J. D., *Lexikon Archaias Hellēnikēs Glōssēs* (*Lexicon of the Ancient Hellenic Language*). Athens: Petrou Dēmētrakou, 1949.

Works by Spiros Zodhiates

The Patience of Hope. Chattanooga: AMG Publishers, 1981.

Editor, *The Complete Word Study New Testament.* Chattanooga: AMG Publishers, 1991.

Editor, *The Complete Word Study Dictionary: New Testament.* Chattanooga: AMG Publishers, 1992.

Immorality in the Church—Can We Sweep It Under the Rug? Chattanooga: AMG Publishers, 1992.

Editor, *Hebrew-Greek Key Study Bible.* Chattanooga: AMG Publishers, 1994.

Scripture Index

John

Acts

Romans

1 Corinthians

2 Corinthians

Galatians

Ephesians

Philippians

Colossians

1 Thessalonians

2 Thessalonians

1 Timothy

2 Timothy

Titus

Hebrews

James

1 Peter

2 Peter

1 John

Jude

Revelation